LALITAMBA

2017

Lalitamba ISSN 1930-0662 is published annually in the United States by Chintamani Books. The journal is a member of the Community of Literary Magazines and Presses. Issues are printed in accordance with the Sustainable Forestry Initiative. For every magazine purchased, a tree is planted.

Submission Guidelines: Please submit up to five poems or one work of prose per envelope. Include SASE and contact information (name, address, telephone, email). Work should be previously unpublished. We accept first North American serial rights. Kindly address correspondence to:

Lalitamba
P.O. Box 131
Planetarium Station
New York, NY 10024

Subscriptions are $12 for one year, plus $4.50 postage and handling.

In the Eastern tradition, spiritual seekers don't take personal credit for offering *seva*, or service. A seeker acts as an instrument for the greater good. This is why we don't list staff names on a masthead. The journal is an offering to the immanent and transcendent divine that lives in the heart, and beyond.

Lalitamba is a 501(c)3 nonprofit organization. The journal is donated to prisons and communities in need throughout the United States. *Lalitamba* also partners with Lalitamba Saranam, a holistic women's shelter in New York City. Proceeds from magazine sales are used for these charitable purposes. Further contributions are tax-deductible according to New York State law.

Website: www.lalitamba.com
Facebook: https://www.facebook.com/Lalitamba-252686692751/

The opinions expressed by contributors do not reflect those of the Editor.

The name for the journal was inspired by a bhajan sung on a pilgrimage through India.

In early 2004, we traveled through the country with India's beloved "hugging saint" to alleviate the suffering that comes with poverty, illness, and plain loss of hope. The journal was founded when we returned to New York City, in November of that year.

The name "Lalitamba" means Divine Mother. In India, the Divine Mother is also praised as jagado dharini, or "She Who Sustains the Universe."

TABLE OF CONTENTS

Essays

Art

LETTERS AND PRAYERS

Alone in the streets, I had no place to go but to God. Now, I want to thank God for all He has done for me.

When I was five years old, my mother told me that I had a problem with schizophrenia and that no one was going to like me, but look at me now. I am 38-years-old with eight children, two sets of twins.

When foster care took my children, I wanted to die, because they are my babies and a gift from God. I love them with all my heart. I pray to God to bless me to be back with my babies.

I was raped at the age of three. That's how I became HIV positive, but my faith in God has healed my body. Then, when I was on drugs and alcohol, He came and healed my body, again.

I pray that you never give up your faith in God. No matter what, if you pray about your family, your relationship, or your job, God will bless you with whatever you need.

M. Pierce
New York, NY

LALITAMBA

I say yes and offer thanks
wondrous effulgence
air after a thunderstorm
woodland edges
stratus clouds, anthelion
above
a clapboard church

I walk the earth
dust to dust
yet in my face
is the breath of life
astral dusk
atomized rain
lambent bird
bittersweet nightshade

Bruce Alford,
Hammond, LA

The journal is an offering.
May all beings be joyful and free.

Ayaz Daryl Nielsen

THE TAO OF BROKENNESS

A broken hub, thirty spokes
without a center
The wheel couldn't turn or
remain upright if
it was needed

The clay pot with a crack
across the bottom would
seep and drip, even
if it was needed

An old homestead without
windows   doors   flooring
or the people to
claim it as home

Empty of emptiness
because of brokenness
non-existence from
lack of usefulness

Each in its isolation
an exhilaration
a clarity
the adventure
of broken existence

Ayaz Daryl Nielsen

UNTITLED

evening wind over the meadow
clusters of blackberry thickets
with meadowlarks, again calling
their notes luminous
my hands are heavily veined,
the skin weathered. . .
and it seems I'm more than I was—
a man, yes
quivering and awake, yes
a man
awake

Hannah Kittle

ASHES, ASHES, WE ALL FALL DOWN

I AM INDEBTED to metaphor.

• • •

I turned thirteen, and I saw red. Red in the tulips that sprouted sporadically throughout the green grass that surrounded our house. Red in the sun, as it sank beneath the dull arrowheads of the distant mountain landscape. Red in the blood of scraped knees and busted lips. Red in the fire that lit our home and burned it to ash piles on the cold earth one late October night.

• • •

The smoke billows and puffs, enfolding each body and object that it can find and touch. Romantic. Through the one-story home it sweeps, reaching its fingers towards the basement and finding an entrance at the top of the stairs in the tiny kitchen. I am fascinated by the smoke. I breathe the gray cloud and feel the pain of a thick rejection. As I crawl on my knees, I feel a deep red seep through my jeans.

I can't see the fire, but I feel the radiance of the heat that melts the walls around me. I didn't set our home ablaze, but I see my contributions falling from the shelves that line the dripping walls. How had I wanted so much? I can hear my dog barking—faintly, muffled, perhaps from outside.

My hands find glass, and I squint to make out the dead red flower that has tipped over with the vase, its pieces scattered and sharp, edged with the vengeance of holding life for no longer than a week: My mother was never any good at keeping plants alive. She killed a cactus once by drowning it.

The floors are becoming unbearably hot against my feet, and my hands are blistering. I try to shout, but the smoke catches my voice. My face smacks the piano bench and swells from the impact, and I find the open door.

The contrast is deep—the dark, star-lit sky masked by a murky white that is far from pure. As I approach my family, I recognize myself in the tears and apologies that rush from my mother. The skilled manipulation that implores an audience, that consoles and comforts, is a natural reflex that I've found exists in both of us.

I quickly cross the lawn and feel the embrace of change in the arms of my parents and my sister. Our golden retriever barks and circles our huddle. He doesn't know what's wrong.

I turn and watch the smoke floating to join the clouds, racing the flames in their wish to touch the sky, defying gravity.

The home begins to crumble. Shattered glass flees the windows with blasts like the sudden unwelcome detonation of an unknown time bomb.

I imagine 70,000 things burning.

All that's left is a foundation with a broken frame.

And the sky looks alive again. A harsh red flickers in the dark night.

• • •

I remember with vividly clear sentiment the feeling of loss that overcame me when my parents sat my sister and me down to inform us that they had acquired a large sum of debt: My mother, unbeknownst to my father, had collected credit cards and thrown them at whomever would accept them. As we sat on the floor, my father explained that $70,000 had gone somewhere, who knows where, and that things were going to be different, that we were in this together.

I could feel the tension between my parents, as my father announced that he wasn't going to leave my mother, that he wasn't going to leave us, but that it was going to be a while before he could trust her again. I don't remember crying or thinking about how hurt I should've been. Rather, I remember sneaking glances at my mother, who sat hunched forward on the couch. Her hands covered her eyes and, every so often, caught the stray tears sliding down her ruddy cheeks.

She looked alone and hurt, because everything she had done she had done to herself. She was caged, caught.

I remember wishing for the conversation to end, for us to completely dismiss the facts that had been spread before us, for us to forgive and forget, sincerely.

• • •

I watch cars slow down as they pass. I see men nudge their wives, while they stare at the charred, cracked walls of my home.

Children point with their mouths ajar, as their dogs hike up their legs in my front lawn.

I stare back.

At a jagged bedroom window, my curtains dance with the outside air.

I watch the house's labored breathing. Its bones shudder. The walls sink slightly, as if exhausted from strenuous labor. The foundation, while still composed, shakes as the pressure builds. The walls are thinning. The dead drywall, or what's left of it, hangs on to create boundaries.

I hear the birds' singing.

I watch the ashes swim, floating and landing on everything that stays still, in the sun rays that flood the open rooms. The walls turn black. The floor turns black.

My books, my desk, my pillows, my clothes. Everything black.

I stand outside with my arms spread wide and gather the flakes, as they drift towards my palms. The sun illuminates my colorless world, sharpening the contrast with the life I wish to know.

I close my eyes.

• • •

I wouldn't say that life became more difficult, just different. I remember finding myself awkward around my mother, not knowing what to say. I walked with a false sense of entitlement, believing that I had a right to feel this way toward her. She had earned my begrudged attitude, and despite the pain that I caused her, I couldn't see past myself to understand that, even though she was my parent, she was still human.

I hated myself for my lack of conversation.

She would hand us dollar bills to buy candy, and I would ask my father if it was okay to spend them. I felt that I had lost a parent, that the person who lived with us was not my mother but a scared woman who desperately wished for her husband to act like her husband again, for her children to act like her children again.

But I couldn't act like her child again. Or maybe I wouldn't.

I didn't share in my father's distrust or my sister's overabundant sympathy, but I, who had always identified with my mother, looked at her face and couldn't see any part of myself in her.

She stood by the open door, begging me to take her money, her dollar bill. I pocketed the cash quickly and escaped through the front door. I offered her distance.

• • •

"Your mother didn't mean to do it. It got out of hand, before she could stop it." My father sits on an old milk crate, and I desperately wish for him not to cry. "We're working hard to fix this place up, but it's difficult. There's just so much that continues to pile on."

"Do you think you can trust her again?" I notice that the basement where we are standing hardly shows damage. The flames were stopped, before they reached here. I find my seat on the rough, carpeted floor.

"I believe so." He runs his hands through his greying hair. "I still very much love your mom." I catch a tear forming and quickly avert my eyes.

"I know."

• • •

In 2006, the nation's consumer debt, when comparing money earned to money spent, towered at a new record of 130.9%. Debt payments made from disposable income broke the record that had reigned since 1980, and families struggled to pay their mortgages on time. Foreclosure notices were highly in demand. Bankruptcy cases became a trend.

In 2006, my mother took a second job at Walmart, where she re-hung bras and underwear near the dressing room in the women's department. My father, and sometimes my sister and I, would drop her off at the front doors and watch her disappear through the automatic sliding glass. I saw her hesitation in slipping on the blue vest that marked her as a Walmart employee and later her relief as she ripped it off on the car ride home. I remember the vest abandoned out of "forgetfulness," as she rushed out of the car. *Or did I imagine that?* I noticed the strain in her eyes at midnight, when I said goodnight.

In 2006, my father made a game out of grocery shopping to see how low we could get the bill each week. One week, we ate for $40.00.

We were never hungry. He worked longer hours as a service technician, and because he worked hard and was good at what he did, he would bring home boxes of free candy bars that had outlasted their shelf life at stores that needed their air conditioning units repaired. At night, he re-routed the electrical wires in our home, which was in the midst of reconstruction.

The church paid off six months of our mortgage.

Anonymous donors paid off our credit card debt.

The ATV was sold.

My allowance disappeared.

My mother found a new job as a social worker, denying and accepting strangers' requests for food stamps.

My parents weren't eligible for government assistance.

• • •

The drywall was hung, replaced. The windows were cleaned and the ash swept away. I sat and watched my mother paint the empty white walls of our entryway crimson red. The paint dripped and puddled in the creases of the plastic, taped down to protect the new wooden floors. Sunlight flooded the room and highlighted her facial features that so much resemble my own.

"You look just like I did, when I was your age." My mother's high cheekbones caught rays of yellow light and shadowed her eyes, eyes that squint shut when she laughs. Wisps of thick brown hair strayed, clinging to her forehead, which was beaded with sweat. A picture frame in the neighboring room holds an image of a woman with two girls straddling the state line. I often mistake this woman for myself.

Up and then down. Down and then up. The brush swept.

While my mother painted the walls red, I adjusted my seat on the floor and distracted myself with the crinkle of the protective plastic. Briefly, I imagined my future, a future consisting entirely of painting walls to hide my misfortunes, a future that streamed images of endless shopping bags and credit cards, a future that exhibited my lack of self-control. I saw flickers of broken glass, crushed walls, burnt memories.

While I watched my mother, I saw the unavoidable truth of myself. I saw where my road would end.

I read my mother's life as a script for my own; her actions and disposition so closely reflect mine that I contemplate her movements, as if they were to predict *my* life and *my* hardships.

The brush whipped and flayed dots of paint that rained onto my face and hands. I wouldn't escape her storm. I forecasted myself in her clouds, because it is in my nature to be like my mother, *to want to be like my mother.* Genetically and emotionally.

I felt the rope around my waist tug and pull me along in the wake of her trail. This is a rope that I tied myself, a rope that awakens me to panic, when I acknowledge that I've woven it myself.

The rope pulled me to recognize that I see my mother's failures rather than her successes, because her mistakes are my mistakes, because her failures are my failures.

Because we are both attracted to fire.

• • •

I became good at keeping secrets. I became good at hiding.

We were in the middle of adding on to our home when, with the new accumulation of debt, all production stopped. For a little while, our inner shambles had been masked by this unfinished house. We had a convenient cover-up as to why our home was in pieces, why we were in pieces.

Eventually, as the house remained unchanged, our mask betrayed us. The windows and doors aged, and the exposed bricks that bordered the window frames peeked from behind the torn drywall, which no longer showed progress, but more closely resembled failure.

Since our excuses were no longer reasonable, neither was the idea of having guests. We found it easier to hide our mess, when no one was around to see it.

At the time, I believed my truths remained unspoken because it was inappropriate to air my family's filthy laundry. It wasn't my place to speak of the tragedy that had brought us to our knees. I wasn't allowed to reveal my parent's pain, their embarrassment.

But that was a lie.

My silence was really about me. My pain, my embarrassment, my tragedy, my awkwardness, my distance, my excuses, my shame, my secrets. It didn't matter that, despite the $70,000 lie, my parents found the strength to hold onto each other, committing to a vow they had taken seventeen years prior. It didn't matter that they eventually crawled out of the burning and consuming debt that had threatened solid ground.

I didn't see the strength in the way my family overcame disaster. I didn't see how my parents became closer because of the struggle that they endured, together. I didn't see my mother's growth, the way she turned her tragedy into a victory.

Rather, I felt shame over her actions, which had brought us to a place where we needed to overcome.

But it was more than that.

I *am* just like my mother, after all. When I look at her, I see my own future, my own terrors. I see my own tendencies through her mistakes and fear that her history will become my own. I see the inevitable repetition of her life in mine, and I know that the path I walked is hers.

So, I buried my truth deep within myself, so deep that not even a fire could smoke it out.

• • •

Red came swiftly that year and took up residence in our home, which did not burn down. Rather, it suffered the fiery heat of a revelation.

I turned thirteen, and I saw red.

Eventually, I stopped running away from my mother, and the red became rich, a rich red that began to heal.

Frank Cavano

CHRYSALIS

many
many many
oh so many
    and
each must pass
through the
terminal
portal but

weep not for
these
chrysalises

hear the
ever-present
singing of
wings

Frank Cavano

UNLESS I ASK A CHILD

Unless I ask a child, I will not know
what wonder is or see a single soul in
a melting pot of faces or catch the
breeze with the fingers of my hand,
then hand it to another's hand.

Unless I ask a child, I will forget to
cry for those less fortunate and see
differences among people as cause for
enmity, and justify my prejudices by
seeing myself as wiser than all others.

Unless I ask a child, I will not recall
the heaven that is within me. I will
live in a frightening world and see it
as my lone reality. I will tremble at a
sudden noise or the onset of a headache.

Unless I ask a child, I will become a
jaded antique, a mere monument to an
absent past, a harbinger of a fearsome
future. Unless I ask a child, I will lose
the very best teacher this world offers.

I will ask a child then, but I shall ask
her while she is very very young and
still functions as life's teacher, for
she will soon be carefully taught by
those who have forgotten, and then
she will forget, unless she asks a child.

Frank Cavano

INTROSPECTIVE

We are what is left after what is said
about us is subtracted.

I am what is left after what I think about me
is subtracted.

I have trouble being honest about myself.
Honestly, I do.

Ego is like the fisherman's catch. It seems to
grow with the passage of time.

With each passing day I seem to be more
stuck on myself. Or am I just more aware
of what has always been so?

Healers are rarely found among those who
write or lecture or advise, but are often found
among those who listen.

I will be still and listen to the wisdom and
the joy of the Spirit.

Desire has many arms. It appears that there is
no end to her goals and agenda. Love, on the
other hand, reaches not for false gods but
knows itself and, in peace and joy, rests
only there.

Life is a tiger without teeth. It scares the hell
out of you, until you make it smile.

Teach and write, write and teach the truth
until, like a good student, you learn it and
live it.

Forgive the past and the future as well, for in
the mind of God, they are gone already.
Offer kindness in the present, and experience
for a moment the heaven that you are.

Be grateful to God, for the Father does not
let the son destroy himself except
temporarily, in his dreams.

Finite mind cannot grasp infinite truth.
I will listen then, to the song that calls to
my heart, and the melody will lead me home.

Devon Balwit

IN THE END, INDIFFERENT

Somewhere on an island with sun and shade, in the midst of peace, security, and happiness, I would in the end be indifferent to whether I was or was not Jewish. But here and now, I cannot be anything else.

—Mihail Sebastian, *Journal 1935-44*

What are we—tribe, blood, imprints of cultural memory,
quirks of parentage, speech patterns, in-jokes, rites peculiar

to each home? Are we never just ourselves and not
all who went before, those corralled, beaten, burned,

made to strip, to shower in unplumbed rooms,
to kneel at the edge of pits, to become crypto or

assimilate? When can we let the ragged standard, the
staggering burden of millennia, fall into the churned muck,

and walk away? When is it no treason not to affiliate,
to claim an individual identity, to be of but not defined by,

to be proud of only what is ours alone? When
comes our time of peaceful indifference?

Eyes of Fire

WARRIORS OF THE RAINBOW

MORE THAN A HUNDRED YEARS AGO, a wise Cree elder had a vision of the future. Eyes of Fire said that there would come a time when the earth would be ravaged and polluted, the forests would be destroyed, the birds would fall from the air, the waters would be blackened, the fish would be poisoned in the streams, and the trees would no longer be, because of the white man's greed. So, mankind as we know it would all but cease to exist.

There would come a time when the keepers of the legend, stories, culture, rituals, and myths, and all the ancient tribal customs would be needed to restore us to health, making the earth green again. They would be mankind's key to survival.

These were the Warriors of the Rainbow.

There would come a day of awakening when all the peoples of all the tribes would form a new world of justice, peace, freedom, and recognition of the Great Spirit.

The Warriors of the Rainbow would spread these messages and teach all peoples of the Earth, or Elohi. They would teach how to live the way of the Great Spirit. They would tell of how the world today has turned away from the Great Spirit and explain that this is why our Earth is sick.

The Warriors of the Rainbow would show the people that this Ancient Being, the Great Spirit, is full of love and understanding, and would teach them how to make the Earth, or Elohi, beautiful again. These warriors would give the people principles or rules to follow to make their path light with the world. These principles would be those of the ancient tribes. The Warriors of the Rainbow would teach the people of the ancient practices of unity, love, and understanding. They would teach of harmony among people in all four corners of the Earth.

Like the ancient tribes, they would teach the people how to pray to the Great Spirit with love that flows like the beautiful mountain stream, and flows along the path to the ocean of life. Once again, we would be able to feel joy in solitude and in councils. We would be free of petty jealousies and love all mankind as our brothers and sisters, regardless of color, race, or religion. We would feel happiness enter our hearts and become as one with the entire human race. Our hearts would be pure and radiate warmth, understanding, and respect for all mankind, nature, and the Great Spirit.

We would once again fill our minds, hearts, souls, and deeds with the purest of thoughts. We would seek the beauty of the Great Spirit. We would find strength and beauty in prayer and the solitude of life.

Our children would once again be able to run free and enjoy the treasures of nature and Mother Earth, free from the fears of toxins and destruction wrought by the practices of greed. The rivers would again run clear, the forests be abundant and beautiful, the animals and birds be replenished. The powers of the plants and animals would again be respected and conservation of all that is beautiful would become a way of life.

The poor, sick, and needy would be cared for by their brothers and sisters of the Earth. These practices would again become a part of our daily lives.

The leaders of the people would be chosen in the old way— not by their political party or who speaks the loudest and boasts the most, not by name calling or mud slinging, but by the truth of their actions. Those who demonstrate love, wisdom, and courage, and those who show that they can and do work for the good of all, would be chosen as the leaders or chiefs. They would be chosen for their character and not the amount of money they have obtained. Like the thoughtful and devoted ancient chiefs, they would understand the people with love and see that the young were educated with the love and wisdom of their surroundings. They would show us that miracles can be accomplished, to heal this world of its ills and restore it to health and beauty.

The tasks of these Warriors of the Rainbow are many and great. There will be terrifying mountains of ignorance to conquer and they shall find prejudice and hatred. They must be dedicated, unwavering in their strength, and strong of heart. They will find willing hearts and minds that will follow them on this road of returning Mother Earth to beauty and plenty, once more.

The day will come. It is not far away.

That day we shall see how we owe our very existence to the people of all tribes that have maintained their culture and heritage, those that have kept the rituals, stories, legends, and myths alive. It will be with this knowledge, the knowledge that they have preserved, that we shall once again return to harmony with nature, Mother Earth, and mankind. It will be with this knowledge that we shall find our key to our survival.

Hopi Prophecy

WHEN THE EARTH is dying, there shall arise a new tribe of all colours and all creeds. This tribe shall be called the Warriors of the Rainbow, and it will put its faith in actions.

Lakota Prophecy

THERE WILL COME a time when the earth is sick and the animals and plants begin to die. Then, the Indians will regain their spirit and gather people of all nations, colors, and beliefs to join together in the fight to save the Earth: The Rainbow Warriors.

Navajo Prophecy

THERE WILL COME a day, when people of all races, colors, and creeds will put aside their differences. They will come together in love, joining hands in unification to heal the Earth and all her children. They will move over the Earth like a great Whirling Rainbow, bringing peace, understanding, and healing everywhere they go. Many creatures thought to be extinct or mythical will resurface at this time; the great trees that perished will return almost overnight. All living things will flourish, drawing sustenance from the breast of our Mother, the Earth.

The great spiritual teachers who walked the Earth and taught the basics of the truths of the Whirling Rainbow Prophecy will return and walk amongst us once more, sharing their power and understanding with all. We will learn how to see and hear in a sacred manner. Men and women will be equals in the way Creator intended them to be; all children will be safe anywhere they want to go. Elders will be respected and valued for their contributions to life. Their wisdom will be sought out. The whole human race will be called the People, and there will be no more war, sickness, or hunger, forever.

Author Unknown

RAINBOW TRIBE

The sun rose on a magical new day.
Over the whole earth they came,
the people of every color,
sister, brother, father, mother,
traveling over many a land,
People of the Rainbow,
Children of the Way,
with a fresh glow
finding their way.
Star within.
More and more joined.
A song for the soul.
A new way to live.
A new way to see.
It happened this way,
and a new song,
it came from within.
If you can find the star
within, then you will find
what is, what was,
and what will be. You see,
it happened this way,
from within.
The people of the Way,
the Rainbow Tribe.

Max West

INTERPRETER OF INFINITY

A lonely toe hold—
tenuous grip
on the mountain tip

I'm an interpreter
of infinity,
which simply means
what's coming from you
is coming from me

Just leaf brushing leaf
as we swing from tree

Max West

ALL THE RELIGIONS ARE WRONG

Either millions upon millions
of people are mistaken
and only one of their gods is right,
or all the religions are wrong
from the moment we began to interpret
experience.

Crystal Berche

ANCIENT OAK DREAMS

If we melt, the world won't notice
I promise
If we take shades of blue
And turn them on their ears
Pickle them 'til they turn pink
And slide them along emerald floors
The illusion of dreams will sit transfixed
In the eyes of witnesses
Who won't bat an eye at the odd children

Crawling through orange rain
The juice of grape soda
Clinging in drops to our lips
Our eyes alight with the glow
Of over-eager mystics bursting at the seams

We dare to dream of scorpion kisses
The burn of a poison caress on mottled snow
Sustaining our pretense of webs and untouchable silence
The dead-eyed doll state of our gaze
Chilling you to your pristine soul

Never trust anything that lives in fear
Of dust and ash and the stink of living
Of a life without kid glove perfection
Of flesh and limb

A cracked mirror reflects the truth of aging
In deep, gouged lines that gape and yawn
You could learn so much from ancient oak dreams
And rings that tell proud stories of storms
And floods and the lean years

When there was little
But that little was everything.

Edward Bruce Bynum

AFTER THE RAIN

After the rain has washed the dust away,
washed the heat away,
washed the morning away,
perfect hands come out of the new air,
rearranging bushes, drying stems,
pulling the concentration out of certain blue flowers.
The roads ribbon out
speaking new cars, new smells,
bright windowpanes, ozone after bursts of clear water
shaken from trees. There are
wheels with cool grease on them,
sacraments of wood.
Irises with all the primary colors practice
opening on the paths you walk.
It is as though someone had been executed,
the bones washed away by the river,
as though we had lived
through the death of a religious tyrant,
were free again
to inhabit god directly, in our own way.
For moments after,
each step is an original adventure:
Each eye blinks a recording of something newer,
greener, wetter, and more succulent
than imagined before.

Dressed in forgiveness, willing to fail,
you launch
out of harbors, where you had been held
by maps of what you thought you knew.
A blackbird on a gravestone glistens,
caws at you, bids you pass on.
Behind you the trails thicken,
fill with subtle beings, noises, loss.

Laurie King-Billman

THIRD ROUND OF THE SWEAT

DRIVING FROM SHIPROCK, I watch the desert sigh into late afternoon. Its mesa-covered back rubs against the dimming sky. I glance down at the hand-drawn instructions that I was given when invited to this Saturday ceremony. They are written on the yellow paper of a lined legal pad. I have grown accustomed to these personalized maps of the Navajo nation, where the GPS cannot reach and regular maps do not stretch. I watch for a sign which proves to be so small I miss it. I get to the *you have gone too far* part of my instructions, a rock formation drawn in pencil entitled "Witch's Hat." Both the drawing and the rock do resemble a pointed hat. The road I take starts wide but soon turns into a twisted path with just enough room for one car driving in one direction, rolling in a cloud of dust.

Finally, I reach the sweat house. It stands in a spot where cottonwoods grow thick. This time of year, they drop their seeds in little white parachutes that look like inflated snowflakes, floating everywhere. A handful float down onto my windshield as I park.

From an adobe house come the smells of fried onions cooking with mutton. I hear ladies' voices, as they put the finishing touches on the stew that will cook for the hours that we face the steam. I wait for them on a wooden bench beside the round, canvas tent, the earth womb we will enter to do four rounds with the steam spirits.

I've sweated once before and gained a healthy fear of how hot that tent can get. Still, the peace I felt from that sweat has made me happy to be invited again.

The First Round

The first round is easy. We are laughing as we file in, women wearing shorts, t-shirts, or swimsuits, women with wrinkled and smooth faces. We sit in a circle on the dirt floor. The hot rocks in a shallow pit in the center have been heating in a wood fire for many hours. I am sitting beside a young Hispanic teacher, and she whispers, "I hope I can take the heat." I am thinking the same thing but do not share this for fear of looking weak. When the flap comes down, our eyes adjust to the dark.

Our leader burns sage over the hot rocks, then pours water onto them. Her gray braids swing as she says a long prayer full of hope for a good sweat.

Introductions begin in the Navajo way, with clan: We name the grandparents who started off our lives. I learn that Sweet Water Clan and Beaver Clan are sitting with Irish Catholic and third-generation Swedish. The teacher beside me shares that her family lived in the area when it was part of Mexico. There are lifelong friends here, mothers, daughters, cousins, and strangers (new to the sweat, like the teacher and me). I learn that we have driven here from all directions: Window Rock, Cortez, Gallup, and Shiprock.

After a bit of light-hearted joking, the leader asks us all to think on what we may pray for during this summer sweat. We sit in silence. The silence ends when she declares an end to the first round and opens the flap, and we arise into a red sunset flaming among the *mesas*. The men who built the fire to heat the rocks earlier that morning come to greet us, and we thank them.

The Second Round

The next round is hotter, and we begin to sweat. Steam moves into our open lungs. One lady prays for a sick child, another for an ex-husband. Six of us pray for drinkers to find their way home. Voices arise in a circle and speak sorrows to the steam. I pray to be blessed with one more child. The teacher prays for patience with her students. We begin to sing—in Navajo, in English, in Spanish; words blend into each other. The steam grows so thick that it seems almost solid. The rocks must be ready to burst into flame.

This is only the second round, yet I feel I will have to leave the sweat tent if it gets much hotter. I do not want to go, to be a weak white woman with these ladies who sit uncomplaining, who have endured so much. So, I hold myself still, do not stand up, try to hang on just a little longer. My prayer now is to be able to face the heat. Our leader, her gray braids loosening, pours more water over the rocks. Scalding steam rises, moving into and over our bodies.

When the flap is opened, the steam follows us out, rising from our glistening bodies. Stars are everywhere.

I breathe deeply. A tight coil inside me has begun to relax. I watch scattered lights come out across the desert. I am surrounded by beauty.

The Third Round

Now, the rocks are so hot that they pop when the leader pours water onto them. A woman my age prays for her grandchildren, for another a lover. We all say a prayer for those drowning in alcohol. We find we all have a drinker who is dying in front of our eyes—a son, a husband, a sister, a mother—people who can't seem to stop, even while they are losing everything.

Vera from Sanoste asks, "Should I stop my love?" No one can answer.

I begin to think of how my life is in its third round. I am middle-aged. My little sack of children-seeds is still ripe inside my navel. I ask the Creator for it to open again, and I see pictures of desert flowers in the back of my eyes through the hot mist. Is this my answer? The steam is a fierce fist of fire pushing down into my flaming chest.

The leader begins a prayer of thanks, and so we all find blessings. To be alive and to have one child may be enough for me.

The teacher whispers to me, "I can barely breathe." Still, she stays.

Women begin to sing "Amazing Grace" in Navajo. Our voices meet in this old tune of redemption.

The heat has become so uncomfortable that I lie close to the edge of the tent. I am hoping for cool air, but find none. Will I lose my dignity if I leave now?

I know that this heat is healing, but right now it feels like a punishment. Finally, the leader declares an end to the round. When the flap opens, the cold air is soft liquid to our throats. An owl hoots as we arise into the night.

We drink water from a tin cup passed around and talk in hushed, reverent voices. We are almost shy with each other for the things shared.

The Fourth Round

More water, fire, and sweat push through our tired bodies. Our leader sits straight and says another prayer. I become convinced that I will have to leave without completing this round. My lungs are on fire, and my eyes burn. The teacher reaches for my hand in the dark and squeezes it. I give her a squeeze back.

It is so dark in the sweat that we have become voices without bodies. A woman tells a secret, and so in the dark, we all tell one. I tell how my dead-before-they-were-born children still pain me. More women speak of their miscarriages and stillborn children. We all say a prayer of acceptance for our drinkers—the only thing we can really do, our leader reminds us. When forgiveness is too hard, we ask for understanding. Fire scrubs angry paths down into our chests. The leader pours more water onto the rocks.

She begins to talk of the day her husband died, killed by a drunken driver. She tells us how she sent her five boys away to boarding school, and she cries. She tells how they all survived these things, and I know I must take the heat.

When the flap opens to our rebirth, I feel the night air, like the rub of fine silk on my cleansed skin. The moon pours its pearl light down into the vast desert. We stand in a circle, as we have sat in the sweat tent. We hug and say the sacred words to each other: "All my relations."

I am ready for what I have inherited, this hard life, now. I must take the heat, hope for four rounds.

We walk together to the house, greeted by the aroma of mutton stew.

Untitled

Katherine West

FACE WITHOUT EYES

The sign was dark against all that white. Two arrows. One pointing straight ahead to the continuation of our trail, rutted and buckled with yak tracks, ski tracks, and the flat pans of snowshoes. The other pointing to the left. To…nothing. The nothingness of looking out over a cliff edge to endless space, endless sky, endless white. There was no trail. The white sky had fallen, covering the ground so that it was as smooth and featureless as its origin. No human had yet set foot or ski or snowshoe to mark human boundaries of organization, ability, and comfort. It was the world before humans. It was the world without humans. A face without eyes. A moon. A moon that sparkled with tiny stars fallen and embedded in its surface—blue stars, red stars, green stars—against white. A moon that hypnotized me, paralyzed me, entranced and enchanted me. I wanted to lie down on it. I wanted to eat it. I wanted to keep it forever. I wanted to slide through it like the forgiving waves of a shallow sea. I put one foot forward, and purity swallowed me whole.

> If I touch you—when
> I touch you, will you change or
> Will the change be mine?

Doug R. Hile

FALL

These are the mornings referred to as brisk,
cold, sharp, and clean. The air stings like a whip,
the sparkling dew not yet frost, not yet crisp,
and a sky as deep blue as the sea.

The creatures have come in the night to partake
of the offerings left in the name of Hecate
to nourish her children, perhaps sweeten a fate
that could use any help there might be.

We all reach a point in the slow march of time
with the days ahead fewer than the ones left behind.
Khayyams' moving finger won't cancel a line,
the Truth for all, there to see.

So savor each day, as it comes in its turn.
Waste not a one, simple lesson to learn
before occupying the funerary urn
or scattering like dust on the sea.

Gunilla Norris

ON THE ROOF

The glow of the city is light years
away. We're on night watch
with nothing much but dark
trusting dark, tender
in the kinship of being.

It's like listening to listening.

No stars. Quiet
unknowing keeps us together
in a gypsy music. One viola
and seven violins.
Infectious laughter. Ache.

All the while the doves on the roof's edge

invite us deeper into night—
a flock of white prayers cooing
and whispering, *Sursum
corda . . . Sursum corda,*[1]
opening their wings.

[1] Lift up your heart.

Mark Ali

ARCHIMEDES' PRINCIPLE

OAKLAND WAS A PORT CITY, and in the darkest of night, in the most silent moments evening produced, he could hear the sound of a buoy calling out to ships carrying their loads.

Often, he was awake during these uneven minutes, these odd hours, so much so his eyes adapted to the dark, as if he had always been draped beneath its murkiness. He was beginning to see through the shrouds and veils clearly now.

He stared at the walls surrounding him, because trying to sleep was wasted exercise. When he closed his eyes, he could feel the stucco partitions leaning in, moving forward, and bearing down.

A swath of moonlight snuck behind the outermost slat of the window blinds and settled high in a corner where edges of the ceiling and two walls came to a point.

The swatch of skylight unfolding on that spot in the room provided a focal point. It was true light in the dark.

No matter how this illumination was affected by the phase of the moon, the starlight that slipped beneath the furthermost slat of the blinds had been there before and stirred something deep within him. Each time his eyes found it, he felt an agitation he was yet unable to resolve, either by flipping his pillow to the cool side or turning over in the bed.

It didn't matter if the sky was clear, cloudy, or overcast. It didn't matter if the moon was young, full, or waning, whether it was hung low or set high. All that did matter was *that* stream of light, which seemed to travel by providence each night to find him.

The light's presence during these awkward hours, these most delicate minutes, allowed him to direct his restless energy to being awake rather than trying to sleep.

The room was pitch-black, save for this light.

Now, his mind was tumbling and traveling, rolling and roaming, swimming and seeking. His thoughts were in a state of gestation, though his form seemed to be in a period of stasis. The visions he was now creating would pull him over the walls of dormancy.

He needed to immerse himself in the world that stretched beyond his window. He needed to be imbued by the soft light commandeering his walls and ceiling.

Those who were completely in the dark would think that he was adrift, lost in the stormy seas of unanchored dreams, piloted by his subconscious fears. They would be unaware of his buccaneer heart, the bounty deep inside, the treasure of his core.

The light was accompanied by the nightly arrival of sounds. These enveloped him. He heard many things—the creaking of the settling house; the whoosh of solitary cars speeding haphazardly; the stretching of tree branches; a dog's spastic barking; the patter-pitter-splattering of rain on rooftops, windowpanes and sidewalks; the burning rubber of screaming tires; and the gunshot's livid staccato.

But it was the gonging bell of the seamark afar that drew his attention. It spoke to him like a West African talking drum.

The port's water was a few miles away, and though it wasn't walking distance from his place of rest, those rolling currents led to a sea of possiblities that lay close to his heart.

He was intrigued that the buoy's sound floated to him every night, just as the light came to him.

Neither were they slaves to bedtime, nyctophobia, or province; for they moved as they were intended too—freely, fearlessly, and without any restraints concocted by man.

Now, the moonlight settled high in the corner of the room. He wanted to travel to where it had been—across the heavens, beyond the waters—to be somewhere other than where he was.

The ringing buoy proved Archimedes' principle[1]: It stayed afloat on the tide, immersed in the sea but never drowning.

Like the buoy, he wanted to negotiate choppy waters, to navigate rough currents and cross seas of discontent; but first, he had to put both feet into the water.

There was a glorious horizon out there. The moonlight on the wall was his North Star and the song of the buoy in the harbor, his compass. He would not remain supine forever.

[1]Archimedes' principle indicates that the upward buoyant force exerted on a body immersed in a liquid, whether fully or partially submerged, is equal to the weight of the liquid that the body displaces.

Michael Salcman

SURREALISM COMES WITH AGE

The world and I are parting
like paper pulled from an etching plate.
Each day comes
in a slightly altered state

as if a smear taken from a glass
or a graphite rubbing made from ancient brass.
Breton loved *frottage* and smoke on a ceiling,
the brown stain of *fumage* in place of feeling.

Today's copy of yesterday whispers of
but cannot touch love's embodied vision
now turned an apparition
I don't fancy very much.

So raise a glass to how much harder I've become,
a half-living moon with its back turned against its sun.

Alexis Ivy

HOUSING

I wasn't there when she took off. It was
the morning shift. She'd told me her new
place was a one-bedroom. Because
all the walls were pine, she'd put up her blue
velvet curtains—And it had a dishwasher. *I swear*
one of those state of the arts. I can't complain.
Trish and Lisa stole me some silverware.

She died doped up, needle still in her vein.
If she'd been here, I'd have called the ambulance.
I would have been doing rounds, seen that she
wasn't breathing. But she was found, body slant
on a mattress, curtains unhung. Free.

She'd finally had it. Housing—
something of a new beginning.

Alexis Ivy

TAKING THE HOMELESS CENSUS

The corner of the laundromat is occupied
by the ex-con with an exhausting past.
He uses missing socks as mittens,
trades them for cigarettes. Homeless:

sitting-on-a-milk-crate homeless,
facial-hair-unkempt homeless,
publically-collecting-cans homeless,
boozing-at-the-duck-pond homeless,
asking-for-the-time homeless.

Teenagers living under bridges, on
benches, or beside the heat vents
in the library. Chronic homeless

who find refuge in the holes of
stairwells. The habitually homeless
who have lived four episodes
of homeless in the past two years.

The girl who stocks the shelves
at 7 Eleven tells me she lives
on her friends' couches. The man
I buy a muffin for at Dunkin' Donuts
Sunday mornings goes south
to be homeless in Rhode Island

all winter. In Public Alleyway
118 three vets have built a room
out of furniture left on the street
by undergraduates. A woman
curled up in a Macy's storefront

doorway leans on the six garbage bags
of her life. On any given night
in January at the Shattuck Shelter,
someone will show up, clean up,
ask for a toothbrush, dry clothes,

five packets of sugar, an outlet,
and then sign in on the sheet
that a bed might be given.
As for the rest of us, uncounted.

Brenton H. Dickson

SEARCHING FOR ANSWERS

ANOTHER FUNERAL. Almost all of my parents' generation were gone.

Gusty February winds swirled recently fallen snow against the large white windows. The smell of rusty steam rose from noisy radiators and drifted through the church. I struggled to get comfortable on the hard wooden pew, while family members and acquaintances remembered the past.

I was thinking more about what would happen next.

My religious friends knew where they were headed after death. Others told me that things just ended, period. I had trouble with both of these outcomes. They seemed much too simple.

At the reception, I was searching for sympathy. (I had just turned 70.) I victimized a friend, Jill. She told me I should read Elizabeth Gilbert's *Eat, Pray, Love*. She assured me that the book would help. My wife Betsy had read the book the previous summer; she'd failed to tell me about it, because it was a "woman's book."

Gilberts's quest for spiritual experience was similar to what I was hearing from my oldest son Brent, a recovering cocaine addict. He'd explained to me with great enthusiasm how he now reached out to his God to help him through each day.

I was shocked. I was certain he'd never been inside a church but for weddings and funerals—except when his younger brother and sister-in-law asked him to be godfather to my oldest grandson.

As a child, I'd had limited exposure to religion.

My mother tried to ease the family's conscience with an outing to the local Unitarian Church every Easter Sunday. I dreaded these trips. My father didn't like them, either. Every year, he would tell my mother, "We aren't being fair. We are selfishly taking the seats of those who worship regularly."

The minister was stern, and he frightened me. He spoke in a loud monotone that droned and threatened. I could never understand what he was talking about. I was sure that he was God or that God was just like him, and I wanted no part of this religion.

Throughout high school and college, I was subjected to required church attendance, in either an established church or the school chapel. My high school and college preachers were uninspiring. I daydreamed and doodled during their sermons.

By the time I was a sophomore in college, I'd found new ways to escape. I would sit in the back of the church, where I would read or do homework.

I discovered that the local Catholic Church simultaneously passed out and collected the attendance slips at the end of each service. (I had been attending at the college's non-denominational chapel, where slips were given out at the beginning and collected at the end.)

A number of friends and I timed our return from the ski slopes to arrive at the end of the three o'clock Mass. We took our seats just in time to receive and sign our "proofs of presence."

I recall one instance when the student monitor, who was handing these out, stared quizzically at my ski boots, the ice still clinging to the lower creases in my Levi's.

I was certain I was in trouble, but I quickly realized he had no intention of turning me in. His nod signaled that an entity far more significant than the college dean was watching over all this, and would deal with me at a later date.

• • •

Decades later, I now wonder whether spiritual experience might be explained scientifically. Academics believe that the brain's electromagnetic field, which transmits radio-like electrical signals to our body parts and instructs us to breathe, walk, and react, is where our conscious and unconscious knowledge is stored.

If this is the case, then when our physical body dies, our brain's non-biodegradable and non-flammable electromagnetic field might remain. It might continue to transmit angry or peaceful signals, or perhaps even knowledge.

I have been telling myself that, being in my seventies, this obsession with finding the truth has been for my own amusement, but maybe there is more to it. Something inside me screams, "I don't want to die."

I try a thought experiment. Maybe, years from now (and I hope it's many years from now), I will return from plowing into fellow shoppers on my electric shopping cart at the local Walmart, look into the bathroom mirror, and see that what my wife calls "good bone structure" will be giving way. My cheeks will have puffed up like popovers; drooping, discolored eye bags will have appeared; my chin will have become indistinguishable from my neck; my teeth will be gone; my hair will have fallen out; I will be wearing high-powered, useless hearing aids; and my eyesight will be failing.

I will grasp at the towel rack to lower myself onto the pot for another bout of diarrhea. At that point, I will collapse into a heap on the bathroom floor.

I will rant. I will rave. I will howl. I will go mad.

Or, perhaps, I will remain standing by the mirror in a state of serenity, grace, and peace. I will smile, because at last I will have comprehended what Elizabeth Gilbert wrote about and what my son has found. I will have spiritually connected with my God.

Unfortunately, this mental exercise does not work. I succeed in horrifying myself, while the hypothesized alternative reaction of peace yet remains elusive.

• • •

In early April I drive to Jaffrey, New Hampshire to hike up Mt. Monadnock. The black flies have not yet made an appearance, though most of the snow is now melted.

I have made this two-mile climb a number of times before with different people—my father, my sister and her husband, my sons, and even a great-aunt.

I scramble up the steep, rocky ascent, over ledges to the summit. I am breathing hard. The muscles in my 70-year-old legs are throbbing. Miles and miles of fields, trees, and villages have unfolded below me. The fresh mountain air is cool and crisp. The sun reflects off of the surrounding rocks.

I close my eyes. I drift into a peaceful and hazy subconscious reverie, back to the numerous times I have stood atop the magical mountain.

This time seems different. My great-aunt Marian's long woolen gray skirt moves gently in the breeze, as if she were pointing out landmarks from her 1890's childhood. She is joking with Charley, my late brother-in-law, who shows no signs of his debilitating Alzheimer's. Just below them, my father runs his trembling hands over a wide vein of white quartz. He marvels at the grooved glacial striations carved into the surrounding granite.

I feel the presence of these others with whom I have made this climb before.

I am not alone.

Naomi Shihab Nye

TURQUOISE DISHES
(In memory, Doris Duke)

Dear Doris
Your turquoise dishes
perfectly arranged on glass shelves
in the Playhouse kitchen—Shangri La

have changed my life
though I will never touch them
or fill them

The tiny cups & saucers
some with lids
some three to a plate
thimble sized
arranged in perfect dignity

Fluted serving dishes
tall pitchers
sleek cups
2 fine fat-bellied pots on the highest shelves
open vases

All ethereal turquoise tone
belonging to air

deep seas
finely fired dreams

Through every sad headline
every breaking news day
these dishes wait

graciously
patiently
for the world to live up to
their calm

Julie Marie Wade

MRS. NEWPORT

[OR A STUDY OF JEALOUSY AS A BLUE-EYED MONSTER]

Mrs. Newport is the mother of Erich Newport, the first boy my mother proposes might be my knight in shining armor. Or, in this case, my knight in gray corduroy pants and two-tone t-shirts. She likes the fact that he never wears jeans.

"But I'm only seven," I protest, after my mother sees the seat assignments at Open House and discovers that Erich and I have been paired for a three-week cycle.

"Mrs. Moak says you get along well together." She is clipping coupons from the paper, and I am coloring at the kitchen table.

"I guess. He shares his eraser and isn't as gross as the other boys"—thinking of Carl Lull and the playground belching contests. Mostly, though, I am jealous, because I have never been asked to join the other boys.

"Do you ever imagine what it might be like to be Julie Newport?" my mother asks, putting down her scissors and smiling.

I'm still trying to imagine what it's like to be Julie Wade.

"When I was your age, we used to write down all the boys we liked and then try on each of their names. It was fun. It was like trying on a new outfit."

She never remembers that I never like trying on clothes.

"Here." My mother takes a crayon—magenta or mulberry—and writes it for me: Julie Marie Newport. "Has a nice ring to it, wouldn't you say?"

. . .

I have told my mother that, because I am in first grade, boys don't interest me much—They couldn't possibly. I'm too young.

But the fact is, I have no short attention span when it comes to Chelsea Brothers, a sixth-grade girl with red curls, pink glasses, and the best kickball kick around. I know I shouldn't be watching. I know my heart shouldn't rattle my chest like an old canteen, then charge up my throat like hungry soldiers storming a mess hall in the movies my father watches on TV. Something just happens to me when we're waiting for our turn on the field and the older kids walk past us, talking easily with each other as if they have nothing to hide, in their more efficient lines. I see Chelsea, and she is smiling at someone so that the freckles bunch up on her nose—a little brown button—and suddenly I forget where I am, forget what I'm supposed to be doing. I forget everything until we play Simon Says or the whistle blows.

. . .

My mother has arranged to have herself invited for tea at Mrs. Newport's house. I will come along and play with Erich and perhaps with his older sister, Shavon.

"I've been dying to get inside that house," I hear my mother say. "She's just so smug about it—as if Genesee Hill is the new hot spot in town and Fauntleroy is some kind of slum."

"I doubt she thinks that," my father replies.

"It's this whole married-to-a-doctor business that gets me. Fine—he's a doctor—but an ophthalmologist. The way she struts around, you'd think he was a cardiac surgeon."

• • •

To be fair, I have never seen Mrs. Newport strut. Strutting is for peacocks and other exotic birds. Mrs. Newport moves slowly, with predicated grace. She has long, thin fingers and gentle hands, which she lays on your shoulder when she asks you a question. I love her soft voice and her glossy clear nails and her signature sweaters, which are light in color and always have a bright blouse with a starched collar beneath them. She wears little gold hoops in her ears and a little gold ring on her finger, and I can't imagine she ever gets angry or dirty, and her skin smells like a fresh peach.

"Remember to be on your best behavior," my mother instructs. "Imagine the Newports are going to be your future in-laws."

"I don't know what that means."

"Look everyone in the face and don't eat too much when snacks are offered."

We ring the doorbell and stand pushing our spines straighter and straighter, my mother in her broomstick skirt and too much make-up, my hair pulled back and braided through with ribbon.

• • •

The Newport house has high ceilings and hardwood floors and a kitchen with an island that stretches almost to the living room. It is open and spacious like houses I have seen in magazines, with windows cut out of the roof and the occasional step up or step down that doesn't belong to a flight of stairs. The white sofa curves around the corner like a cat's flexible back, and the bookcases are built into the walls and covered with glass.

"Welcome," Mrs. Newport smiles. She wears lavender slacks to match the lavender blouse beneath her gray cashmere sweater. "Erich and Shavon have just returned from ice-skating lessons, so they'll be down just as soon as they've had their showers. The tea is steeping and in the meantime—" she lays a hand on my shoulder and bends toward me so as not to tower—"what would you like to drink?"

I glance at my mother, then reply. "Nothing just yet, thank you. I'll wait to see what Erich is thirsty for."

"All right, then. Shall I give you the tour? Would you like to see the rest of our little cottage?"

I am about to observe that this isn't a cottage at all—more like a mansion or perhaps a *chateau*, though I am less certain of the latter word's requirements. My mother pinches my arm, intercepts me quickly: "Yes, of course, Jan. We'd love to."

• • •

Later, Erich and I recede to his room, where we drink Capri Suns and find we have less to say to each other outside of school.

"Do you have any pets?" I ask, following his example and sitting cross-legged on the plush blue carpet.

"We used to have a cat named Daisy, but she ran away when we moved."

"Oh," I nod, sipping the passion fruit juice, while my eyes wander the length of the walls. "Our mailman has a daughter named Daisy and another daughter named Lily. I always think it's funny that cats can have people names."

"People can have flower names," he remarks, "so I guess cats can, too."

This observation makes me smile, and I wonder if Erich Newport is one of those "still waters that run deep," an expression I have heard my father use before. In fact, Erich looks a little like the pictures I've seen of my father as a child—a gap between his new front teeth, a handful of freckles garnishing his cheeks, and blondish-red hair cut close to his scalp, with bangs that resemble a girl's. Erich is also "tall and husky," as my mother says, and she has mentioned before that he looks like he'll be "a natural on the football field."

"Do you play sports?" I inquire.

"Yeah," he says. "I'm an ice skater."

"That isn't a real sport—is it?"

"Sure it is. Didn't you see the Winter Games?"

I shrug and tug on my straw. "The ones in Japan?"

"Well, you've seen figure skating before, right?" he says.

"I guess so."

"Who do you think holds the women up? The men have to be really strong." He seems emotional now, his face flushing as he explains.

I nod. "That makes sense."

"Do you want to go out back and play on my swing set?"

Erich Newport is lucky. Imagine having a swing set and a sister.

• • •

When he opens the closet to find his shoes, I notice that the top shelf is filled with Care Bears. From my vantage, it seems that there must be more than a dozen of them, all crammed together, a few even upside down.

"I love Care Bears," I say. "I only have one, though. The one with the rainbow on her belly."

Now Erich's face turns the color of bologna, and he slams the door shut in a hurry. "You aren't supposed to see those."

"Why not?"

"Just—" he paces the perimeter of the room now, nervously— "my mother doesn't want anyone to know I have them."

"Are they hand-me-downs from your sister or something?"

Erich is a bad liar. He looks to the side, then away as he answers, "Yeah. They're mostly all Shavon's."

• • •

At home, my mother serves French dip sandwiches, which we don't often have. I wonder if we are celebrating some kind of victory.

"Did you have fun, Smidge?" my father asks, covering his tie with a napkin.

"It was okay," I say. I want to tell him about the Care Bears but sense I shouldn't, sense it will give my mother an unpleasant source of power.

"The house is nice—if you like that kind of floor plan," my mother concedes. "It's clear his practice must be going well."

"Eric and Shavon take ice skating lessons," I say. "I thought ice skating was only for girls." This is how I test the waters.

"I used to ice skate when I was a boy," my father replies, "but there weren't any lessons. What's to learn? You go down to the lake, put on some skates, and have a go at it."

"They skate at an indoor rink—like roller skating, but with blades instead of wheels."

"Isn't that kind of nancy?" my father asks, raising his eyebrows at my mother.

"Bill, trust me. Erich Newport is 100% boy. He's probably just taking those lessons so Shavon will have someone to go with." Now my mother turns a diligent eye in my direction. "You know, it wouldn't hurt you to try some ice skating lessons. I think it helps with posture and balance, and coupled with ballet…" Her voice trails off, and I know she is suggesting something I don't quite understand. I imagine it has to do with the awkwardness I feel in my own body, the shame that falls over my face each time the other girls sink down into the splits, while I sit high and straining.

"Did you see Jerry?" My father's voice is hushed, as if hoping I won't hear.

"No. I guess he was at the office, but I did think about your sister while I was there."

Now, I am listening more keenly than ever. "What about Aunt Linda?" I want to know.

My parents exchange a furtive glance. "Well," my father says at last, "your Aunt Linda went to high school with Jerry Newport. They were in the same class."

"Was he her boyfriend?" I ask.

"They were just friends," my mother replies too quickly, eager to change the subject. "Now make sure to eat some of your salad."

• • •

The next year in school, we have a man-teacher, and I try to keep an open mind about it. After all, if Erich Newport can ice skate and collect Care Bears, Mr. Whited should be able to teach second grade if he wants to. On his desk, he keeps pictures of his daughters, and sometimes his wife brings him lunch in a Tupperware container he heats up in the communal microwave. Although he seems nice on the surface, Mr. Whited also has a dark side, a temper that stretches out like seaweed and tangles your legs as you try to swim past. Like my mother, you don't want to make him mad.

Lana Steeley must not realize she is taking her life in her hands—all eight years of meticulous self-construction—when she passes a note to Erin Sauter during Language Arts time. I watch the sheet of blue-striped notebook paper slide from palm to palm, listen for the crinkle as Erin unfolds the top, the sides, the little isosceles of the secret.

Suddenly, Mr. Whited is upon her, seizing the note in his huge white hands, holding it up like a victory flag. "Well, well, let's see what we have here—" in the slow, detestable tone of a movie villain. "Isn't this interesting?"

He turns the paper around so the whole class can see. It is a blue-ink drawing of a bed with tall posts and two heads propped up on the pillows. "The caption here reads—" He is taking his time to increase the suspense, to heighten Lana's pink-faced horror. I wonder if the lights will flicker and Mr. Whited be found slumped on the floor. "—Lana and Lee, naked in bed." Gasps and giggles from around the room. "So this is a picture, in case we weren't sure, of Lana Steeley"—pointing to the girl-head with pigtails and bows—"and Lee Bennett"— pointing to the boy-head with spiky hair—"*naked* in *bed.*"

Why would they be naked? I wondered. *Had there been a fire? Had something horrible happened to their clothes?*

"Where are you in this, Erin? Are you taking a Polaroid picture?"

"I didn't know what was in it," she says, her hands retracting into the sinkholes of her sleeves.

"Lee, it looks like you have a not-so-secret admirer," Mr. Whited proclaims, carrying the note across the room and placing it dramatically on the desk of the boy beside me. "If I were you, I'd have this picture framed. Hang it up on your bedroom wall like a pendant."

Lee's face doesn't flush, and his hands don't tremble. He keeps his eyes firmly glued to the floor.

"As for Miss Steeley, she and her friend Miss Sauter are going to spend today's recess cleaning out the rabbit cage. And tomorrow's recess. And recess the day after that."

I look over at Lana, whose small face is wide and red as a camellia, whose eyes have pooled into two dark puddles of tears. Is it the note she regrets or only the punishment?

"And if I catch anyone else passing notes in class, you'll have to stand up and kiss the subject of your note in front of everyone." More gasps and giggles. "Then, you'll have to clean the rabbit cage."

By second-grade standards, this is a scandal. I want to tell someone, but I have to be careful about choosing the right person to confide in.

• • •

"Shall we go outside and practice our jacks?" Aunt Linda suggests. She is teaching me the game with the little red ball and the strange silver pieces that look like you could fold them together into miniature jungle gyms. On my grandmother's driveway, we sit down and savor the early spring sun.

"I have a question," I say, after I'm sure we won't be overheard.

"Okay. I hope I have an answer." She has put her sunglasses on, which means I won't be able to scan her eyes to assess the truth of any response she provides.

I want to tell what has happened, to simply recount the events, but I sense somehow that I need to ease more slowly into this subject—like using the ladder in a swimming pool instead of leaping from the ledge. "Well, it's about boys," I begin. "How do you know if you like a boy?"

"I guess you want to spend time with him. You watch for him, and you notice when he's not there."

"What if you're glad he's not there?"

Aunt Linda laughs now and stretches her legs in the track pants that crinkle like tissue paper. "Then, I guess you don't like him very much. Or—maybe you feel shy because you do like him and are relieved that you don't have to try so hard that day."

"So, how do you know if a boy likes you?" It is a good strategy, I think, because soon I will reveal that I'm asking on behalf of Lana Steeley, who got caught drawing naughty pictures in class. Maybe she was trying to get Lee to like her.

"Someday, if they like you, boys will be able to tell you to your face. It's harder now, because they're still figuring out who they are." This is a feeling I understand so well that I am filled with sudden compassion for boys.

"So why don't girls tell them—to their face—if they know?" This is important. This is going to be my seamless segue to Lana Steeley.

"It's not very lady-like," Aunt Linda sighs. "It's better to let the boy make the first move."

What I mean to say is that Lana Steeley might have wanted Lee Bennett to like her, but since she couldn't tell him to his face, she had to find another way—embarrassing, yes, but undeniably certain. A spilled secret, maybe worth the rabbit cage.

Instead, out of nowhere I say, "Did you like Mr. Newport in high school? Did Mr. Newport like you?"

The jacks scatter from Aunt Linda's hand. "Mr. Newport?"

"Jerry Newport, Erich Newport's dad."

"Where did you hear about that?" she asks, running a hand through her frosted hair.

"Nowhere. I mean, you just hear things. Did he ask you to a dance? Did you ever pass notes about him in class?"

"No." She shakes her head and fiddles with her zipper, so that I won't see the splotches on her throat. "Nothing like that. People can know each other—they can be acquaintances without—" The little red ball lodges in the grass. "Always remember," she says, lacing her Reebok sneakers with her un-ringed hands, "not every story is a love story." Her voice becomes softly oracular. "Most stories are anything but."

I decide to make a list of every kind of story I know. There are love stories of course, and fairy tales, and murder mysteries, and other kinds of mysteries where no one dies. Is that it? Is that everything?

I twist my brain into knots tighter than snarled hair or too-small sweaters, but I can't come up with anything else.

• • •

The next year in third grade, we study cursive writing. Once we've learned to make all our letters by tracing from the workbook, Mrs. Moak distributes large sheets of paper with a blank space at the top and lines like train tracks passing through the rest of the page.

"Today, you're going to write a story," she says. You can write about anything you want, but you have to use cursive letters. When you're finished writing, you can draw a picture to illustrate your work."

Erich Newport is once again my random-assignment seat mate. In quiet defiance of the rules, he takes out his Crayola kit and begins with his picture. In the far left corner, he draws a tall brown building with lots of windows and a sign on the lawn. In the far right corner, he draws a house with a chimney puffing smoke and a long driveway with a car parked near the end.

"Julie, eyes on your own paper please," Mrs. Moak instructs.

"What story are you going to write?" I ask Erich, as I sharpen my pencil with protracted care.

"I'm writing a true story," he replies. "It's about my family and how we have to live in a hotel, until they finish construction on our house."

"You're living in a hotel?" I whisper, incredulous.

"Uh-huh. My mom says it will take at least two whole months to finish the master bedroom and the rooftop terrace."

I glance over at his paper and notice a large round of blue in the center. "Is that a lake?" I inquire.

"No. That's the swimming pool my parents are putting in."

• • •

This information is too much for me to contain. At the dinner table, almost before my father has finished the prayer, I burst out, "The Newports are going to have a swimming pool in their backyard."

"Well, you have a swimming pool," my father replies, "though I guess you've all but outgrown it by now."

"Not that kind of swimming pool," I say. "Erich told me all about it. They're living in a hotel, and they have bulldozers digging up their backyard and everything. It's going to be built into the ground, like the pool at the Southwest Community Center. They're even going to have a hot tub and an outdoor shower."

My mother's eyes narrow, and she inspects my face for any trace of insincerity. "This sounds like a whale of a tale to me," she replies.

"Call Mrs. Newport," I challenge. "See for yourself."

My mother regards me for a moment, then her corn on the cob and butter knife in hand. Finally, having made her decision, she stands up, strides over to the phone, and begins to dial a number.

I wait with baited breath while my father puts down his fork and happily peruses the paper. He knows he's not allowed to read during meals, but my mother's absence from the table constitutes a brief intermission.

"Jan?—" a pause, and then, on a note of moral indignation— "Figures they would have an answering machine."

As she listens, my mother jots down a number on one of her recipe cards, then returns to the table, a troubled expression on her face. "It seems the Newports have temporarily relocated to the Holiday Inn. Here's a number where they can be reached," she says, waving the card like a little white flag and frowning.

I smile and rock in my chair. "See? I told you. Erich lives in a hotel, now. They're building a swimming pool. It's all a true story."

Not only is this story true, but for some reason, it is particularly upsetting to my mother.

When I bring home the invitation to our end-of-year party, she takes the yellow paper, masterfully stenciled with beach balls and picnic baskets, and crumples it, tossing away the invitation that reads: Come join us for a celebration of your child's successful completion of third grade. This year's party will be hosted by the Newport family. Students should bring swimsuits, towels, and a change of clothes, as it will be a swimming party. Parents are requested to contribute a side dish or dessert.

"You know I've always wanted a swimming pool," my mother snaps, slamming the basement door and loudly securing the lock.

"You can still have one," my father assures her. "It's not like there's a limit on the number of pools or a shortage of people to hire."

I climb out of bed and move quickly to the threshold of my room, listening as their conversation unfolds.

"But now it's ruined, Bill. Don't you see? It's not our special thing anymore. It's the Newports' thing. Why is it always the Newports?"

"I don't think—"

"Jan Newport never worked a day in her life, and here I am doing the reading program and tutoring for the schools. You know that's what I wanted to do with the money." She is stomping her feet, which makes the chandelier in the dining room shake and the china in the cabinets wobble.

"No one's stopping you," my father replies. "Why are you making this a competition?"

"Oh, that's rich. I'm making it a competition. I'm bragging to everyone about how we just remodeled our house that we only bought two years ago." She starts to cry, and my father cannot console her, and before long she is calling him names and telling him that he should go and live at the Holiday Inn. This prospect pleases me, provided I can go with him.

Later that night, propped up on my lacy pillows, I commence reading a Crowell biography of an important woman named Jane Addams. This new genre of true stories is what we have been assigned to read for our first-ever oral book reports. In addition to reading and writing about the person in question, we are required to stand before our peers and present what we have learned to the class.

• • •

"You know," I tell my Aunt Linda, "you remind me a lot of Jane Addams. She was a very nice person. She liked to travel, and she never got married in her whole life. I'm not sure if she even had a boyfriend."

We are sitting at my grandmother's kitchen table, she with her cup of coffee, I with my glass of milk. Aunt Linda offers me a wan smile and glances at Grandma, who is playing solitaire and listening as we talk.

"Jane Addams received the Nobel Peace Prize," my grandmother offers without looking up. "It's a remarkable honor, particularly for a woman."

"You were alive then weren't you, Grandma?"

"Yes, I was. I was about twenty years old, as I recall." She smiles at me, then chews her dry toast contentedly.

"Did you know Jane Addams?" This possibility intrigues me, and I nearly catapult from my chair at the thought.

"No, no," she chuckles, "nothing like that. But I did know of her and of all the good work she did at Hull House."

The tight lines in Aunt Linda's cheeks have loosened now, and she suggests that I present my book report for them. "Be sure to read slowly and clearly, and to pause now and then to look people in the eye."

I stand up, smooth the wrinkles from my paper, and commence with confidence. "Jane Addams was an important American woman, born in 1860. She lived for 74 years but always had a lot of health problems. Her father encouraged her to go to college, even though that wasn't typical for women of her time. Not only did she go to college in the United States and Europe, but also she never got married or had any children, which would probably have made her father really sad, if he hadn't dropped dead suddenly when she was still a young woman."

When I stop to breathe and make eye contact with the audience, I catch my aunt and grandmother exchanging circumspect looks.

"After that, Jane Addams inherited money and started having a lot more fun. She traveled with her stepmother and her college friend Ellen Starr, and throughout her life, she had a lot of lady friends who lived with her and helped her to help others. She seemed to like Mary Rozet Smith best of all."

My grandmother raises her hand, a gentle stop sign in the midst of my speech. "You know, dear," she says, "I think you might not want to focus so much on Jane Addams' personal life. Your teacher likely wants to know why she was honored with the Nobel Peace Prize—what service she performed, what organizations she belonged to. It isn't really relevant whether or not she was married or how she spent her private time."

"But isn't that why she could do all the good things she did? Because she didn't have to cook dinner every night for her husband and change her children's dirty diapers all the time?" This is the hypothesis that has been forming in my mind—that if you want to be important as a woman, you need to forego the traditional path.

I think I see the faint curve of a smile pass over my Aunt Linda's lips, but she looks down at the crossword page and says nothing. My grandmother's reply has the quiet ring of regret. "Well, every woman serves in her own way. Whatever else, you must remember that."

• • •

My mother has made tinker cake and sliced it into several dozen pieces. She has wound her hair with hot curlers, lifted hand weights in her bedroom, and put on a pair of white pants with gold thongs and a Hawaiian shirt layered with large wooden beads. I wear my swimsuit under my clothes and wince as she pulls my hair back into a headache-inducing ponytail. Since I'm going to be playing in the water, she says there's no point trying to make me look good; decent is the best we can do.

"Remember to be as gracious as possible to Mrs. Newport. Compliment her on the changes they've made to the house, especially the swimming pool. The last thing we want her to think is that you're jealous." Her blue eyes are almost bright enough to burn.

"Don't worry," I tell my mother. "I'm not jealous. I think it's too cold to have a swimming pool in Seattle anyway. A hot tub would be pretty nice, though."

• • •

When we arrive, Mrs. Newport greets us warmly, offering to take my bag and stow it away in Shavon's room. "We have two bathrooms on the main level and another upstairs," she says, leaning in to address me directly. "You can change wherever you feel comfortable, and when you're ready, head right out to the pool."

"I am ready," I say, peeling off my shirt and shorts and handing them in earnest to my mother.

Mrs. Newport smiles, her face the same color as her thin cardigan and matching slacks. It is a color I think they call mauve.

"Well then, off with you," she exclaims, gesturing toward the sliding glass doors.

"Oh, by the way," I call over my shoulder, imitating the housewives I've heard on TV, "I love what you've done with the place."

• • •

The swimming pool is shaped like a kidney bean, with warm inlaid bricks around the edges and shiny blue tiles along the interior wall. The sides and bottom resemble a bath tub—toothy-white, almost like porcelain—though to the touch, the surface feels rough, nothing sharp or jagged, but nothing you could slip on, either. The hot tub curves into the pool on one side, with a slot in the blue-tiled wall where steamy water cascades in a constant waterfall. Soon, I have lost myself in a cannon ball contest with Erich and some of the boys.

When Mr. Newport comes home, it is time for hot dogs, which he cooks over the grill. His sleeves are rolled up, and his shiny blue tie is still on.

"What do you tell Mr. Newport?" my mother nudges me from behind.

"Thank you—for the hot dog and for letting us swim in your pool. It's really the best pool ever, even on a cloudy day."

Mr. Newport is shorter than my father, and his hair is darker, though I see he has started to go gray along his sideburns.

"It's our pleasure," he replies. "What's the good of having these little luxuries if you can't share them with other people?"

As my mother begins to inquire about length and depth, landscaping work, and choice of tile, I wander into the house to look for cookies.

When I see Mrs. Moak, she hands me my report card and wishes me well in fourth grade. "You have a lot of spirit," she says. "Now it's time to work on harnessing your potential and directing it toward the most fruitful outcomes."

I nod, not understanding, and tear open the envelope—our first report card of letter grades. There is an A in Science, another in Math, another in History and Geography and Physical Education and—"Mrs. Moak?"

She turns back mid-bite, her hot dog dripping with relish.

"How did I get a B+ in Language Arts class? Words are my favorite subject."

"You're good with language," she tells me, "and you have strong reading comprehension skills, but Language Arts also includes your penmanship and your book report, both of which"—she hesitates—"aren't quite up to snuff."

"What is snuff?" I plead. "Nobody ever told me what snuff is."

"It's just an expression, dear," Mrs. Moak says, her face softening. "It means that you haven't learned how to follow the pattern precisely, yet. You tend not to follow directions, even when they are very clearly given."

• • •

I pass the refrigerator on my way to the bathroom, the tears like hot lava inside of me. Mrs. Newport has already put Erich's report card on display—seven perfect A's, like arrows through the bull's eye of the page.

Suddenly, a streak of anger—or is it something else?—pre-empts my sadness. No one sees me as I tear it down.

I look around, sure that someone will intercede. Outside, the adults are eating and chatting, and the children are still playing in the pool. No one is watching as I climb the stairs stealthily, taking two at a time. In the master bathroom, over the well-scrubbed toilet bowl, I shred our records, his and mine. Then, I lean on the silver handle and flush with all my might.

EPILOGUE:
FOURTH GRADE END-OF-YEAR PARTY, SOUTHGATE ROLLER RINK

Erich Newport doesn't do well on roller skates. It turns out wheels are harder for him than blades. Lee Bennett and I have been skating together all afternoon, but now he's gone off with Marissa Sheldon in search of soda, and I can't find a trace of them anywhere around the concession stand.

When I slump down beside Erich on the brown carpeted bench, we nod at each other, affirm our mutual discontent, rub our skate-wheels on the rug, and brood in silence.

Finally, he says, "I hear your parents put in a swimming pool."

"Yeah," I tell him, "it's true."

"I hear it looks just like ours. I mean, exactly. Down to the last detail. Down to the shape and the size and the blue rim of tile."

There is no use denying this. "Yeah. It's like they had a copy machine."

To my surprise, he doesn't get mad, doesn't pick up or scoot away. "Do you like it?" he asks.

"Well, it wasn't my idea in the first place, and to tell you the truth, I think I liked the grass a little better."

Just then, Mrs. Newport steps through the doors, pushing them open like the passage to a pantry. Her hair gleams gold, then silver, beneath the disco-ball light, and she waves to Erich from a distance, motioning for him.

"Don't tell my mom," he says. "It would hurt her feelings, but to tell you the truth—" he looks at me squarely now—"sometimes, I really miss my swing set."

Jennifer Newhouse

FOOTBALL

A boy rushes the unknowable field.
Then another. Mothers sit
in lawn chairs, looking on.
From this angle, each body
is the size of the moon, full. The moon
streaked black with sky and night.
America, is this your story? Blue and red
Walmart windbreakers
cutting into the abyss, shifting—
invisible—into night? The mothers
with hand-held plastic fans looking on?

T.R. Jones

BEHIND THE WHEEL: A RECOLLECTION

IN 1980s TEXAS, a learner's permit was much more than a simple card. It was a symbol of liberation, as meaningful to aspiring drivers as the Magna Carta was to 13th century English barons. I received that sacred piece of paper on the final day of my freshman year, and I knew it to be the most important document ever spit out by a dot-matrix printer: proof that the State of Texas deemed it prudent for an uncoordinated, ADHD-addled 15-year-old to climb behind the wheel of a ton of steel and plastic and zip down public roads at speeds much too slow for him, much too fast for everyone else. It was also my ticket into the behind-the-wheel component of the driver's ed program, which began the week after school let out.

That first day, I was full of nervous energy. I found it nearly impossible to pay attention while my instructor, a monstrous, six-foot-four, 400-pound football coach, droned endlessly on about this knob and that pedal and blah blah blah. When he squeezed into the passenger seat of the school's Ford Taurus, I had to bite my lower lip to keep from laughing—It was like watching a circus elephant climb into a clown car.

Then, we were on the road, and my amusement yielded to the desire to drive.

Oh, the exhilaration. My life would never be the same. Being behind the wheel completed me, as if a part of my soul had been missing for the last decade-and-a-half. Naturally, I resented it every time I had to give up the driver's seat to one of the two mousy girls who made up the rest of my group. After all, I'd turned out to be a prodigy, a master of vehicular navigation, and the driver's seat was where I belonged.

Our corpulent instructor undoubtedly agreed. He was forever gasping in awe at my ability to dart nimbly in and out of traffic, for my expertise often left him speechless. It was surely clear to him after our first session that I needed no further instruction, and he made me continue only because he didn't want to deprive himself of the experience.

I'm sure that he was devastated when the final day rolled around. The huge grin plastered across his face was merely his way of hiding it.

While I was enjoying my last turn behind the wheel, we approached an awkwardly constructed switchback that emptied into an adjacent highway, and he indicated that I should take it. Conventional wisdom dictated that I slow down while rounding the tight curve, but I knew such nonsense only applied to amateurs.

Heedless of the 15-mph warning sign, I pushed it to 40 before pulling the steering wheel hard to the right. The NASA-worthy G-forces pinned me to the driver-side door, and so as all good drivers know to do, I hit the brakes. The rear end of the bulky car fishtailed through the last few yards, and for a moment, I became a wee bit concerned the car might flip onto its side.

Apparently I wasn't the only one concerned, because a shrill scream suddenly assaulted my ears—a scream so full of terror you'd have thought that there was an axe-murderer in the back seat.

Trying not to feel insulted, I peered into the rearview mirror at the girls in the backseat. We were safely on the highway now, but both of them still clung to the handholds above the windows. Despite the adrenaline crashing through my veins, I felt a twinge of remorse.

Not bothering to return my eyes to the road, I said, "Sorry. I didn't mean to make you scream."

After a heartbeat or two, one of them answered, "Um, that wasn't us."

Then, with one hand still clutching his door and the other planted against the dashboard, the wrecking-ball of a man sitting next to me squeaked, "That was me."

Somehow, I still passed.

Korkut Onaran

OVERHEARING THOSE AROUND ME

Flip flops and the feet:
It's like paying attention—
It's like this, this, and this!
I mean, it's not a real job.

The flowering street tree:
I am realizing more and more
that I need to celebrate myself
as an artist.

The tree grate:
It's not like I don't have
a business model. I can
channel myself, manage my rhythm.

The loud black SUV driving by slowly:
I am falling into a silence so deep
I don't remember anymore
what my ears are for.

The green tea leaf floating in my cup:
The day is tender.
There are flecks of gratitude
in the air.

LALITAMBA

The clashing orange-and-peach
pattern on the woman's tights:
I really don't want to
not be all over
this opportunity.

Hot pants:
Could you take a picture of us,
together? Be sure
that the building shows at the back as well.

The clock on the building wall
across the street:
I come here to watch people.
You know—
It's crazy!

Patricia Farewell

THE VISIT

So you have come when I am not myself . . .
These fingers cannot reach your outstretched hand.
You say there is more to life than good health?

Remind me, dear, how happy I once felt.
Use simple words; I want to understand.
I tell you again I am not myself.

This illness tracked me with relentless stealth,
upsetting what little I ever planned.
Tell me, is there more to life than good health?

My body . . . are there words? . . . I have no breath
to say what's on my mind. I'm an old man
you visit when he is not himself.

I cannot make sense of what I've been dealt.
My thoughts whirl uselessly like grains of sand.
You say there is more to life than good health?

Was that you at the window when darkness fell?
Was that you, tall and still, your long arms tanned?
I wish I were able to be myself.
Tell me there is more to life than good health.

Candace Lyons

THE DINNER

"Can't. I dine with Peter Blanchard tonight. How about next week?"

"Okay. Who's Peter Blanchard?"

"A friend. You don't know him." Lily doesn't add, "Neither do I," but suggests a time and place to meet with Kit. "See you then," she says before Kit can bring up Peter Blanchard again.

Lily is pleased with herself. There's no way she's going to tell Kit, or any else, about Peter Blanchard. Not yet, at any rate. Not that she thinks there's anything wrong with him, at least she hopes not. It's just that she'd have to explain how the dinner came about and that's a subject she'd rather avoid.

• • •

Placing a personal ad was something she'd done during a fit of the blues when she hadn't cared if she lived or died, but had desperately cared, on the chance she continued living, that it would no longer be alone. Once the tidal wave of hormones had receded, she couldn't believe what she'd done. She'd managed to put it out of her mind until someone from the newspaper called and requested she pick up her mail.

This someone had been so insistent that Lily had expected bags of letters and was surprised there'd been such a fuss over the handful of envelopes that awaited her.

"Maybe he had the blues too," Lily told herself, as she stuck the letters into her bag and took them home, trying to decide whether to read them, throw them into the trash, or wait until the next high tide of hormones made having placed the ad seem like a good idea again.

Curiosity won out. Lily tossed the letters onto the desk, instead of into the wastebasket, and later that same evening brought the stack into the living room.

"Okay guys, humour me," she said. The importance of humour in a relationship had been the subject of Lily's ad. She thought she'd hammered the point home, but obviously she'd been too subtle. Humour was singularly lacking, and several letters actually made her nauseous. Apparently, there were a lot of disturbed people out there who turned more than crude when protected by the anonymity of the mail.

Lily unfolded one sheet of paper to find a message composed of words and images cut from a magazine—short, sick, and highly pornographic—that made her grateful for her own anonymity provided by the newspaper's post office box. The G-rated letters weren't much better. Rather than try to amuse her, their authors had desperately tried to impress her with how cool, smart, or sexy they were.

"Sorry," Lily thought, "but I'm not convinced. God's gift to womankind doesn't need the personals."

Peter Blanchard's letter wasn't the last in the stack. It was merely the last she read. She'd gotten so discouraged that she promised herself this would be the last she read, as she opened the envelope.

Inside was an index card on which he had written, "Me too." That was it, except for his name, address, and phone number. It was a response to the last line of her ad: "I'm not looking for my one true love. I'm just looking for someone who can make me laugh."

Peter Blanchard had done it. Lily was chuckling out loud as she put the card aside. She scooped up the rest of the letters, read and unread, trying to think of an appropriate manner—hanging, dismemberment—to dispose of the pornographic suitors. Finally, she dumped all of their letters into the trash bin and then washed her hands.

Lily returned to contemplate the index card. "Okay, Me-Too, where do we go from here?" she wondered aloud.

Lily wasn't sure. In theory, Peter Blanchard had fulfilled his role, and she could let things end right here. Yet, she stuck the index card in the frame of the medicine cabinet mirror and stared at it through at least a dozen toothbrushings, before making up her mind.

Actually, she had the sickos to thank for her decision. Lily wanted to know more about Peter Blanchard, but only if she could maintain as much of the anonymity that existed between them as possible. The phone, she concluded, was even more anonymous than a further exchange of letters.

She hung up on Peter Blanchard's answering machine three times before she actually got hold of him. She'd almost hung up again but found the courage to blurt out, "Hi, this is Lily, the woman whose ad you answered." Then, she kept talking fast, something she did well when she was nervous, not mentioning her last name, hoping this oversight would go unnoticed.

They chatted a little. Peter Blanchard didn't make her laugh right away, but he did provoke a smile or two. The conversation was awkwardly pleasant, and Peter Blanchard was honest, for he suggested, "Maybe we could dine and that way, if the evening's not a great success, at least we'll have had a good meal."

This did provoke a laugh from Lily, but it was his saying "dine" rather than something like "grab a bite to eat" that made her say yes. Dining meant that Peter Blanchard was interested in getting to know her, whereas grabbing a bite would have meant that he was actually interested in grabbing Lily at the earliest opportunity.

Still, when he asked for her number in case there was any need to change plans, she gave him her work number without mentioning it as such.

Peter Blanchard said he'd make a reservation at Caspar's in his name, so that they wouldn't have to worry about recognizing each other. Lily found this an excellent idea.

Caspar's wasn't chic, but it wasn't a place for her habitual jeans either, and she was going to have to buy a dress.

• • •

The dress has been bought. It lies on the bed waiting for Lily to put it on, but she's not due to meet Peter Blanchard for a few hours. Lily wishes she were the nail-polish-and-full-make-up type, so that she'd have some way to kill the time. She debates calling Kit back, yet further questions about Peter Blanchard seem inevitable, and so Lily tries to read instead.

Every few paragraphs, her concentration wanes, so she puts the book aside, attends to some long neglected chore, and then tries to read again. Finally, she puts the book aside for good and begins to pace.

When she gets to the bedroom, she asks the dress, "What am I doing?" She picks it up and stares at it, as if waiting for an answer. When there is none, she plunks onto the bed, while still holding onto the dress. The cloth is sympathetically limp in her hand. "I do not want to go on this date," she tells the dress, and is dismayed by her bad timing.

Until this moment, Lily hasn't thought about the dinner, except as an appointment on her agenda like a trip to the dentist. She's picked a lousy moment for important revelations. Not only does she have to think this date over, but she's got to think it over fast.

Lily smoothes the dress out, abandons it on the bed, and goes to do her pacing in the living room where she can roam more freely, but it's still not enough space. When Lily needs to think, she needs to walk not pace, so she puts on her jacket and hits the streets.

"What's the problem here?" she asks herself, to get things started. The answer is simple. The problem is that this date is a major mistake. She should never have submitted her ad or responded to Peter Blanchard's letter.

"Okay, hot shot," she chides herself. "Why is this date a mistake?"

That question stops both her feet and her brain, because Lily isn't even sure which question to answer. She decides to take things chronologically. *Why the ad?* Simple again—temporary insanity, a legitimate legal defense.

She manages to get her feet moving a bit more quickly along the street as she risks the tougher question. *Why had she decided to call Peter Blanchard?* The answer awaits her several blocks away: because she'd read all of those other letters and had been presented with a world full of sex maniacs and dweebs.

Stumbling upon Peter Blanchard's letter had restored her faith in humanity. She'd acted upon it. Okey-dokey. This is progress.

Lily picks up her pace and heads into the park, where the hardier flowers persist among the fallen leaves. The place is pretty, and Lily is beginning to relax, when the big why presents itself. *Why doesn't she want to keep the date?*

Lily sits down for this one. Actually, she slumps against the park bench, hands in pockets, legs stretching halfway across the path, and contemplates the knees of her jeans. They're getting dangerously worn, she notices with a sigh.

These are her favourite jeans. She's trying to remember where she bought them, when she realizes she's lost her train of thought. She stands up and sets out on her way again.

Why doesn't she want to keep this date?

"Because," she thinks, and then she continues to think without getting any further. She's tromping along with the sound of the thought *because* setting the rhythm of her stride.

She looks around to see where she is, finds that she's looped around to the front of her own building, and goes up to the apartment.

She pulls out a sheet of paper, writes "because" at the top, and starts a list:

1. I don't know this guy.

2. I don't like blind dates.

3. I'm not hungry.

This third notation she scratches out. There's no time for jokes.

3. I was not in my right mind when I took out the ad and cannot be held responsible.

Lily is tempted to cross this out, too, for it's an excuse and not a reason, but she decides not to. It's a good excuse.

Lily sits staring at the paper, yet the list does not grow. She realises that her list is flimsy. She should be leaving in half an hour. For want of a good reason not to, she goes into the bathroom to take a shower and pull herself together.

• • •

Lily is bent forward, brushng her hair in front of the full-length mirror in the bedroom. When she straightens up to flip her hair back into place, she gives her reflection a critical glance. The dress is actually becoming. She likes what she sees.

Lily has never considered herself more than reasonably attractive—perhaps pretty on a good day. This turns out to be a good day. She tries to be pleased that she has somewhere to go, since she looks so nice. It always seems like a waste when a good day comes along and she's got no plans. She slips on her shoes, puts on her coat, and heads to the door.

Her hand is on the knob but neither turns.

Lily herself has turned to stone, or so it feels.

If someone appeared behind her and put a gun to her head, she'd have to let him shoot.

She knows she cannot make herself go any further.

Lily doesn't attempt another round of rationalizations. She returns to her bedroom and takes off the clothes that she's just put on. When she's down to her slip, she sends herself to bed without any supper.

And Peter Blanchard? Peter Blanchard dines alone.

Ivan de Monbrison

TRANSHUMANCE

Adossé à la colline la route qui divague nous mène à l'aire
du saule pleureur près de la mare où nous nous asseyons
pour dormir un instant.

L'été de grande sécheresse a cousu nos lèvres sèches du fil
de la pensée.

La terre vacille sous nos pieds fourchus comme nous
repartons en fin de journée en direction de la mer que nous
devinons par-delà l'horizon.

La nuit qui vient pas à pas marche sur nos talons et a tôt fait
de nous rattraper dans sa course.

Notre marche s'accompagne d'étoiles familières comme
les constellations. Orion. Les Pléiades.

Nous arrivons bientôt à l'aube et fourbus par notre périple
nous nous asseyons pour éloigner quelques pensées
maudites qui nous assaillent.

Bientôt, en rêve, l'enfance revient nous donner son bonjour.
Nous sommes jeunes à nouveau, en rêve nous revoyons notre
mère, jeune elle aussi, qui nous surveille de loin dans
nos jeux enfantins. Il y a ces amis disparus depuis bientôt
quarante ans qui nous reviennent, nous les retrouvons
dans notre mémoire comme si c'était hier; comme nous sommes
travaillés par la lumière de l'été, assoupis à l'ombre
d'un micocoulier.

L'esprit agrège le temps au temps.

Le chien de notre enfance est mort depuis longtemps.
Toison d'or, jeux, courses dans les herbes folles.

Foisonnement de choses improbables, comme la trace
laissée dans la matière par le reflux du ciel et qui réjouit
notre insouciance blanche tandis que nous cheminons
sur la route qui serpente entre les collines.

Parvenus au rivage nous pouvons deviner que la journée
sera chaude. Le bateau dans la rade est déjà reparti. Il est trop
tard pour prendre place à son bord; notre indolence demeure
notre seul refuge. Le silence sur la terre attrape et
retient au passage le soir qui passe.

Quel chant nomade te donnera la vertu de savoir découvrir
l'intelligence secrète des choses?

Ces nattes pour dormir te sont offertes, l'orbe de la lune
blanche est posé sur ta bouche.

Sous l'arbre qui somnole nous avons vu la pensée divaguer
en ses rivages pluvieux. Nous avons contemplés les jachères
inaltérées de notre enfance. Nous avons donné au sommeil
l'aumône de notre foi.

Telle est la tendre patience dont dispose le mort
qui nous est familier.

L'âme bleuit dans la nuit.

Le poète le connaît et l'appelle tout bas.

Ivan de Monbrison

TRANSHUMANCE (ENGLISH TRANSLATION)

Up against the hill, the wandering road leads us to a wild spot
by the willow tree near the pool, where we sit down
to sleep for a while.

The drought of the summer has sewn our dry lips up
with the thread of thought.

The earth wobbles under our forked feet as we rise up
and leave at the day's end, heading for the sea which we guess
lies beyond the horizon.

The night comes up walking on our heels and soon enough
has caught up in its rush.

Our stroll is busy with stars, familiar as the constellations
can be. Orion. The Pleiades.

Our journey ends at dawn; exhausted, we sit to leave aside
the cursed thoughts which assail us.

Soon, in a dream, childhood returns to greet us. Once again,
we are young. In a dream, we see our mother also young,
watching our games from afar. We reunite with friends
gone forty years now. We see them in memory, vivid as if
we had left them only yesterday; exhausted by the blazing light
of summer, we try to sleep beneath the shade of a hackberry.

Mind aggregates from time to time.

The dog of our childhood has been dead for a long time.
Golden fleece, childhood games, wilderness romps.

Here arise the proliferation of unlikely things, like the mark
left in matter by the low tide of the sky, a delight for our
pale recklessness. We tread the wandering road between hills.
As we reach the shore, we guess that the day will be hot.
The boat in the creek is leaving. Now, it is already too late
to board the boat; our indolence, our only shelter. Silence
over the earth has caught and holds the passing evening.

What nomadic chant will give you the virtue to discover
the secret intelligence of things?

These mats set out for sleep are a gift for you;
the orb of white moon alights on your mouth.

Under the drowsing tree, we have seen thought raving
amid rainy shores. We have considered the unaltered fallows
of our childhood. We have given to sleep the alms of our faith.

Such is the tender patience which the dying man has at his
disposal, he who is familiar to us.

The soul turns blue at night.

The poet knows the soul and calls it quietly.

Irfan Merchant

PANCHGANI

I want to walk again those winding lanes
through *peepul* trees to where my heart finds rest
and land to root itself: another home
to house that self that only knows
the pulse of song, the ecstasy of rain.

Calcutta, India 1980
Mark Wyatt

Calcutta, India 1980

Mark Wyatt

Kathmandu, Nepal 1980
Mark Wyatt

Kathmandu, Nepal 1980
Mark Wyatt

Hainan Island, People's Republic of China 1995
Mark Wyatt

Eliot Hudson

DANCING IN AUSCHWITZ

One can note a sort of decay in the confidence placed by the two last centuries in the idea of progress...I use the name Auschwitz to point out the irreverence of empirical matter, the stuff of recent past history, in terms of the modern claim to help mankind to emancipate itself...So there is a sort of sorrow in the Zeitgeist. This can express itself by reactive or reactionary attitudes or by utopias, but never by a positive orientation offering a new perspective.

—Jean-Francois Lyotard

"SHHH...WE'LL WAKE THE OTHERS." Anna blew out the candle in front of the shimmering icon, and the room went dark but for a moonlit sliver cutting down the corridor. Death has a curious way of bringing the living together, and had her Grandfather not gone the way of all flesh, I'm sure she would not have found solace in our own. I felt lost, but beyond the shores of her gown, I'd found the coast of her soul.

"I'm sorry. I could not tell you in the light, because I was ashamed, but you can't be nice to me." She paused and continued, "It will be very hard for me not to like you. You can't be sweet to me." Then, she kissed me.

Her nails were painted black for her friend's wedding, just as she had entered my life wearing all black to commemorate her grandfather. My books and lecture papers were in Scotland, as were our work uniforms, green aprons, and coffee scented laundry.

The moon shone through the curtains and bathed Oświęcim (that place the Germans named Auschwitz) in a buttermilk light. The floor gave a little with each step.

Outside, the wind picked up and murmured, wafting smells of *kiełbasa* and garlic from the kitchen, and the clock struck that midnight hour of neither yesterday nor tomorrow.

Her glasses rested upon her nose. When she pushed them up, they sparkled in the dim light of the street lamps that lined the walkway between the late-Communist high-rises, outside. She held my arm and whispered, as we navigated the hall's shadows.

"You cannot make me love you." She pulled me closer. "Because you're leaving."

"I have to go back," I said, and we entered the room of her childhood.

"So, you cannot be mine."

When we spilled onto the bed, she touched my cheek with her hand. Quiet and soft. I looked into the lenses of her glasses and longed to read the future, as though they were shattered bits of a crystal ball.

"Then, what are the rules?" I asked, brushing the hair from her face.

"There are none. This isn't language."

"And I cannot be yours?"

Mystery hid in the dusk of her crevices. Her bottom lip jutted out slightly, and she pulled me closer into her.

• • •

The following day, Anna gave me her late Grandfather's slippers to wear for the Easter meal, and I shuffled into the dining room, in the shadows of his footsteps, and sat down at the table.

"...For those who cannot be with us...rest their souls...to sing your praises...with Christ who died and now lives...*in nomine patris* *et filii et spiritus sancti...*Amen," Anna translated the prayer with closed eyes. Wisps of brown hair fell lightly over her nose.

She tucked her hair behind her ear and waved her fork, as if it were a baton calling forth a melody of fish and bread. The food rose and fell in swells of pickled fragrances and meaty aromas. She summoned the baritone of her father's laughter over the percussive clinks of silverware upon porcelain in a waltz without time. Somewhere, the fragrance of mustard arose, as did that of the caramelized onions in sour cream.

Then, the faces at the table turned as sour as the cream.

"They're asking if we will marry, but they already know the answer."

Anna began whispering, "неТ, неТ," and I understood that although we'd shared the same years on this spinning rock, she'd grown up with sauerkraut and a Soviet Wolf, one who smoked cigarettes and wore bell-bottoms, while I'd grown up with Doritos and the Lion King.

Either that realization or my own vulnerability drew me to her. I felt strangely naked without language to clothe me.

Anna's father, thin as the cigarette he lit, signaled to his wife. She thundered back, shaking her head, but he protested.

She lamented, lifting her bulky frame, and waddled to the cupboard on the wall. She pulled out a bottle without a label and gave it to Anna's father, who removed the cork by gripping it with his teeth and rotating the glass. He handed the bottle to Anna.

Anna poured the dark red spirit into the glasses placed around the table.

I shuffled my feet inside a dead man's slippers, while ten Polish eyes gazed at me.

"We say На здоровье."

"Na Zdorovie," I resounded.

We all tipped our glasses back, and I looked toward heaven. Anna smirked, her lips tightening. Her chest fluttered with a giggle, and the family laughed, too.

Curious, my eyes begged the translation of their laughter, for whether sinister or playful, even laughter has an accent.

"My grandmother laughs at you because, if you don't look everyone in the eye when you drink the spirits, then you have seven years bad—um—luck."

The grandmother's smile was wide, showing her gums. Her dentures were tucked into a napkin upon the table.

I scratched my head and narrowed my eyes "But I'm dating you—Your grandmother's laughing because I'm going to have bad *luck* with you?"

The grandmother roared and pounded the table with her glass, then drank more wine. The family continued to howl, wiping tears from their eyes.

When the grandmother drank, she smiled, so that she looked pained. The shadows of her eyes sank into the hollows of her sockets, as if she were a skull jesting in the dark.

"На здоровье."

"This is wine made by my grandfather." Anna sipped the spirit of her dead grandfather, then covered her mouth with the back of her hand to cough. Beneath the table, she extended her fingertips and brushed the top of my hand. Light settled at the bottom of her glasses, highlighting the curved frame.

As I cut into my potato *pierogi*, Anna asked, "So why did America go crazy?"

"What?" I turned toward her. I swallowed the *pierogi* and then put down my fork.

"I am speaking for my father. He ask, 'If America's so smart, then why they go crazy?'" Anna translated as the medium, with her eyes rolled back. "Iraq, Afghanistan, Vietnam? They were so smart? But, Rock and Roll. Gospel, Jazz, Blues, Motown. My father says only the insane can make music so good."

Her father rapped the table with his fingers. One leg was draped over the other, and his toe tapped up and down, as if it were playing along to a song no one else could hear.

The grandmother now led the conversation, as she pointed a finger, riddled with age and twisted with arthritis. She spoke through Anna: "Because of Auschwitz, in Oświęcim for a long time, we couldn't have any *discotheques*, any bars, any life. They thought we weren't allowed to, like we didn't live here before Nazi's come. Afterward, we lived in town but were supposed to not have color and just pray. Everyone else in world could dance to new music, but not us."

"Who are *they*?" I asked, drinking the spirit of her grandfather.

"People not from here. Still, for most people, Auschwitz and Oświęcim is the same. They don't see the difference between them. I think how long the old generation is still alive and how long they want only keep it as place where a lot of people died. We have to respect their wishes, but I have to say you see changes, like Festival of Life, to break the spell of the town and let us live, too. In Oświęcim we're beginning to dance again."

I set down the glass of wine, spilled the spirit of her grandfather all over my *pierogi*, and almost broke the glass. The commotion jarred the family, who held their breath and looked at me.

Luckily, there is an Easter custom in Poland of throwing water at one another while crying out, "Smigus Dyngus." I lifted my fork with one hand and ate a wine soaked *pierogi*. I reached my other hand into a cup of water, and began tossing droplets at the family and shouting out, "Smigus Dyngus."

They shrieked, batting away the water with their hands while embracing it with their smiles.

Then, Anna shouted back, "'Smigus Dyngus' is only for tomorrow."

That night she lay with her back to me.

"No, not anymore," she said.

I was tidying the room, folding my clothes like little ghosts, tucking them one on top of another, neatly into my suitcase.

"What?"

"I have to be emotionally invested, and you're leaving."

· · ·

The wedding was held at a church an hour away, where houses were so distant that the settlement remained nameless. We drove down forked roads, cutting and twisting through evergreen forests with the smell of wood burning fires. Bones and ambiguous forms of tufted kill littered the road. Rivers whispered to the birds that held the sky beneath their wings. When the birds were tired of gathering in the sky, they came to rest upon the gables of a nearing church, which was our destination.

"We're here. I remember it just the same as when I was little," Anna said, touching her reflection on the car window.

The dilapidated church appeared abandoned. Green paint peeled from the onion dome. Some of the shingles were missing from the sides, though the building still retained a semblance of warmth, like that of an old man whose unshaven cheeks yet harbor the affections of a smile. There was a cemetery with moss burying the gravestones. Upon the sole steeple were four clocks, one clock to each side, and each face told a different hour.

Anna smiled at the flower girl, who skipped down the aisle in spasms of unbridled enthusiasm, like a new lamb, as she scattered white rose petals.

"I need to ask you a question, but you'll laugh," I whispered, trying to hold her hand in the pew.

"You can't need me." Anna pulled her hand away.

The bride stepped delicately, swaying like the flowers whose petals were strewn across the church floor.

At the altar, the groom stood as if the prime of his life were tucked into his vest pocket.

A recorded voice played, and Anna whispered, "Papież Jan Pawel." She wore a band in her hair. A flower blossomed from the temple of her crown, and she touched the flower.

"Part of me really wants to be mad at you, and the other half is hurt by you. If there were any other parts, then I'd just want to get away…" she whispered. Her knees were bent, so that the toes of her high heels touched the floor.

A red and beige fresco painted on the church wall depicted scenes of Oświęcim throughout time. Knights, Turks, castles, and prisoners were portrayed.

Waiters relocated the pews to the transepts of the church, as they set up for the reception, to be held within the nave. The tables, prepared in the sanctuary, were carefully brought in.

From the treasury, white-gloved waiters delivered three-tiered fruit-platters, the plates silver and the handles crystal.

Fiber optic lights glowed pink, yellow, and green over the dance floor.

"You look beautiful," Anna said, straightening the lapels of my suit. Then, she touched my throat and brushed my hair.

Toward the wall, there was an ice sculpture of two lovers waltzing, the girl in an elegant fluid dress which rippled outward, the man clutching her hand.

"Is yours cold?" she asked me.

"Yes."

She brought the bowl of *borscht* to her lips and tipped the soup into her mouth.

The ice sculpture melted slowly.

The booze began to hit me, and the room seemed to pour like vodka. The soldiers on the wall aimed their guns over the heads of the musicians. Stained church light tickled the muzzles of the saxophones. A girl rapped a wooden drumstick upon an electronic drum, sounding a cadence that made the room vibrant.

Everything drifted into itself, blurring past, present, and future. Tenses became little more than a grammatical fabrication, a thin veil revealing the movement of time itself, dancing.

"I don't like our future together," she said.

The mural depicting the Berlin wall was crumbling. Citadels collapsed around the bride and groom, who threw their champagne flutes over their shoulders.

The glass shattered on the floor, beneath the eaves of the ruinous church, and scattered like stars upon the night.

Shards of glass danced toward us, as we sat before prisoners depicted in striped clothes, disrobing and then naked. They ascended to the top of the ceiling, where birds gathered in flight.

The musician's violin trilled. I leaned in toward Anna, and I held out my hand.

"What is point?" she said, looking at the time on her iPhone. Then, she sipped red wine from a crystal glass. Behind her, the armor and lances of Turks in turbans emerged from rows of soldiers on horseback.

"Please?" I caressed the small of her back.

She grabbed my arm and dug her nails into my skin.

Along the western wall, stained glass Stations of the Cross allowed sunlight to move through the church, gracing the white veil of the bride's head, turning it crimson.

"No. I don't want," she said.

A cavalry of knights galloped across the wall from the east.

I offered my hand again, and this time we drifted to the dance floor in the glow of soft pink, blue, and green lights. We lingered in a caress, rising and falling with the melody, and she shuddered.

"I love you, but don't love me back." Her touch begged my silence.

"How long does this song go?" I asked, and she stroked my cheek, closing her eyes.

"Don't ask these questions," she whispered.

I could feel her lips brush my ear.

She trembled, as if she were dreaming. The fiber optic stars painted shadows on her eyelids, and we shuffled like two skulls touching one another, just bones swaying in an embrace, the well-tailored dress of our flesh clinging to our ribs.

We danced to a lullaby of the things we'd never said.

I coiled in the darkness of her crevice, while we whispered kisses and eyelashes, and she twisted as women do.

Outside, it began to snow. Bits of white burrowed into the grass, as though the sky had been shot down, the snow nothing more than shattered bits of alabaster walls and delicately broken belfries, glimmering shards from the kingdom of God. Falling *bastilles* flickered as they glided to the earth to rest upon the sod where we buried our dead. Heaven had turned to glistening pieces, fragments of perfection we happened upon, if we were lucky.

So we walked in midnight's footprints of forever's eve, and she smiled, mysterious as superstition. Her fragrance was softer than remembrance, her breath a whisper, fainter than recollection.

And all at once, nothing but the mute pulse of the earth.

"I love to hear you breathe," she said.

Selected Artists

GIFT OF LOVE

URI BULGARIA COMMEMORATED World Interfaith Harmony Week 2016 at the National Palace of Culture in Sofia. The National Palace of Culture hosted the intercultural student exhibition Gift of Love for the period 11-20 February. The event was organized by Bridges—Eastern European Forum for Dialogue Cooperation Circle (URI Europe) in cooperation with the Center for European Refugees Migration and Ethnic Studies (CERMES) and the Bulgarian-European Cultural Center.

The interfaith project Gift of Love displayed art works by 35 students from two Bulgarian Universities (New Bulgarian University and Veliko Tarnovo University). Works included sculpture made from glass, wood, and stone; paintings; and photography. Each of the works manifested young people's understanding of love for "the other" and for "our neighbor."

The official opening ceremony took place on 11 February at 18:00 and began with the lighting of the National Palace of Culture in purple (to celebrate the United Nations' Interfaith Harmony Week).

More than 150 people of various backgrounds were present during the official opening: religious leaders, diplomats, European Parliament members, university professors, journalists, and students. Christian Orthodox, Catholics, Protestants, Muslims, Jews, and atheists gathered together. The deputy Mufti Biraly Mumun was among these guests.

"Art is one of the strongest tools in interfaith and intercultural dialogue, and love is a supreme gift given to human beings," were the opening words of Angelina Vladikova, Chair of Bridges.

"Interfaith harmony and tolerance are very much needed today. We must educate our children and cultivate tolerance, because it is part of the understanding of harmony," added Miroslav Borshosh, Director of the National Palace of Culture.

"We consider culture as a forum, as a transformer and changemaker, innovating and experimenting and establishing new room for dialogue with the audience," concluded Professor Anna Krasteva (CERMES), in her speech of gratitude to the National Palace of Culture.

The event was held under the special patronage of Mrs. Mariya Gabrielle, Bulgarian MEP, Vice-Chair of the Group of the European People's Party in the European Parliament.

Frozen Strength
Alexander Tasev

Divine Beginning
Aleksandra Veleva

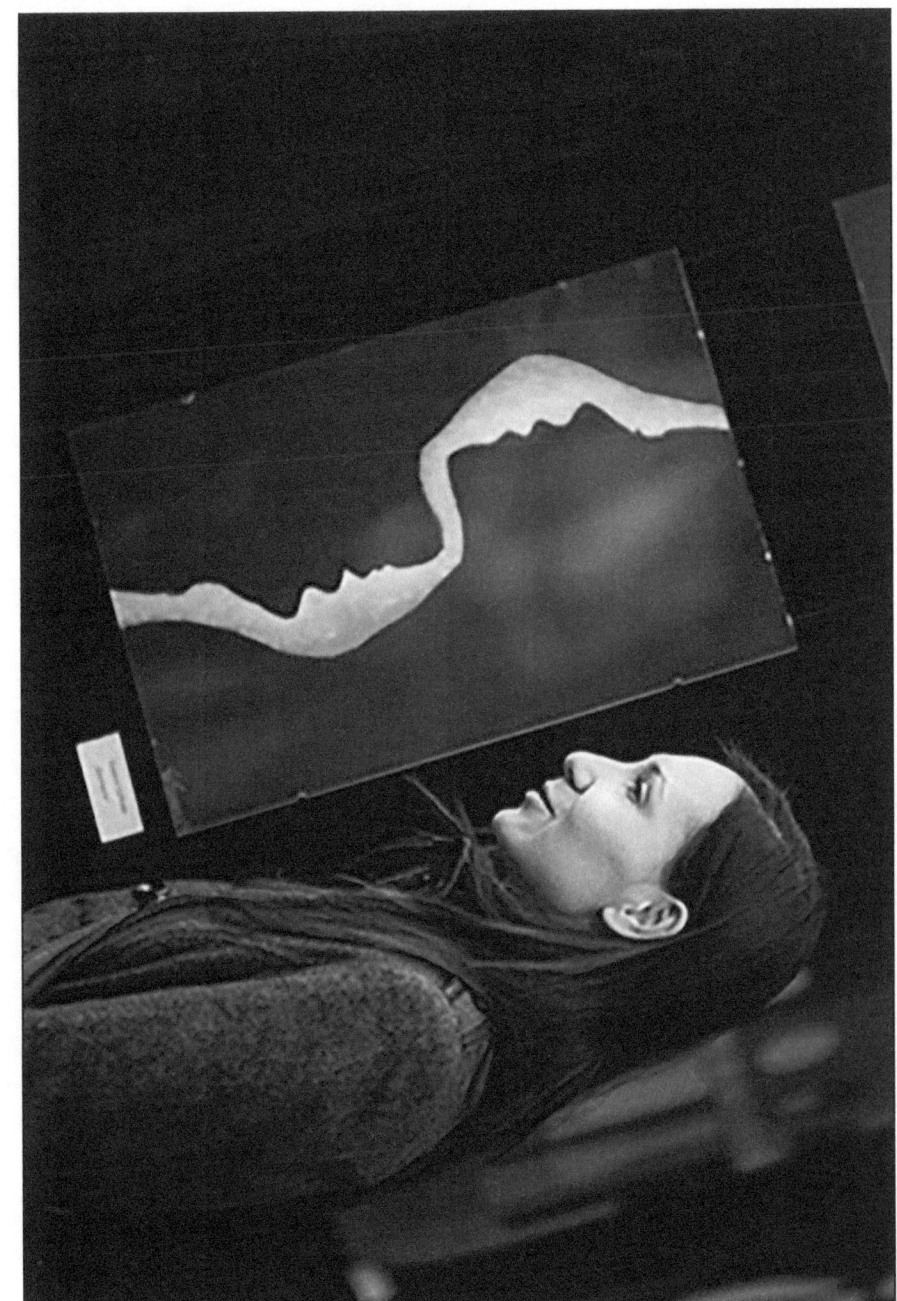

Different

Borvana Bobeva

Cosmic Wormhole

Tanya Hubenova

Joseph Rathgeber

I AM A PALESTINIAN [4]

and *There is no such thing as a Palestinian people.* I am
dispossessed. I am Mahmoud Darwish. I am Leila Khaled.
I am Handala. I am Naji al-Ali. I am a cartoon character.

I am a refugee in the cross-hairs of an assassin. I am Edward Said.
I am Ghassan Kanafani. I am your friend. I am Husni Daghash.
I am still in exile. I am an orphan after the massacre

at Deir Yassin. I am the Nakba. I am Ghada Karmi. I am
Rachel Corrie. *I write it out in verse.* I am the PLO, the PFLP.
I am the Intifada. I am the *fedayeen.* I am the shepherd's sling.

Melvin Sterne

HARIJAN

THE MATTRESS IS OF COCONUT HUSKS—the cheapest mattress the world has ever seen. It is a poor man's mattress, the husks not even broken and woven into fiber, just stuffed into a hand-stitched, oversized burlap sack. The locals say that coconut husk mattresses support the posture, that the coconut itself has cooling properties, and that, at the very least, it discourages bedbugs. "And sleep," Father Juricich sometimes adds, on the nights when he lies on his back, the husks digging and aggravating his old war wounds. "A mattress is also for sleep."

It's two o'clock in the afternoon, the hottest part of the day, and Father Juricich should be napping, but a myriad of distractions keep him at the brink of—but unable to slip over the edge into—sleep. At first, it was the mattress. Then it was the ceiling fan rattling and grinding as it stirred the desultory air of his room. Then it was the obsessive notion that the fan was about to come unfastened and fall onto his bed below—not an impossibility given the age of the fan and the condition of the ceiling.

He got up and shut off the fan, but the room grew hot. He kicked off the covers. He rolled over. He rolled back. He turned the fan back on and pulled the covers to his chin. Finally, he relaxed, allowing the sound to hypnotize him. The drowsiness he craved melted into his consciousness, like a teabag steeping in warm milk.

And then, Father Juricich felt the sting of an insect. Thereafter, his skin was hyper-sensitized, and he felt like he was being eaten alive. Finally, he prayed, mindful of his human frailty and mindful of the suffering of the martyred saints. They before him had undergone infinitely worse. Father Juricich offered himself as a living sacrifice to every hungry mosquito and biting fly passing through the neighborhood, and then he gave up.

At length, he sighed, eased out of his bed, and slipped into his black *kurta*. He had long ago abandoned the official priestly garb in favor of an Indian-Western hybrid.

He checked his watch and smoothed the pages of the diary on his desk, but before he began to write, he opened his bedroom door and looked into the front room for Shunita, his housekeeper.

She was gone, to market or to do the laundry. So, Father Juricich lit the burner on the little gas stove and made his own coffee, grinding the beans in a hand-cranked mill mounted on the wall, then boiling the grounds in sweetened milk and straining them out of the finished coffee through a cheesecloth. Before he could drink, there was a knock at the door.

Two boys stood on the steps outside, wheezing and panting, as if they had run for some distance. It took Father Juricich a moment to recognize them. They were from the Nair family, a large clan of devout Hindus. They were not on the list of regular callers the priest might have expected.

"Come, come," shouted one boy. The other echoed, "Come, quick. There has been an accident." He placed extra emphasis on the final word *accident*.

Father Juricich squinted up at the sun, which was beating straight down onto his garden. He prayed inwardly that he wouldn't have to walk far but knew intuitively that he would. He scolded himself for this self-indulgence.

"Just a moment," he said.

He partially closed the door and went into his room. There, he slipped on his sandals, made a mental note to take a bottle of water, found his old and well-worn traveling Bible, and then, forgetting the water, returned to the boys.

Neither of the boys spoke English well, and when Father Juricich inquired in his broken Malayalam what the matter was, they both jabbered excitedly, such that Father Juricich couldn't make heads or tails of what they were saying. Nevertheless, they took him by the hands and rushed him along.

Father Juricich tried to oblige, forcing his long legs to make up in length-of-stride what he lacked in footspeed. He tried to imagine what sort of catastrophe might have brought the Nair boys to his door, with the most likely scenarios being that some foreigner had OD'd or become ill or suffered misfortune in one of the city's back alleys, or that a dispute had flared between Hindus and Muslims over a business deal gone bad, or that a son and daughter had been caught in indecency, or some other such rubbish that might call for a neutral adjudicator.

Whatever the problem might turn out to be, Father Juricich was sure it would have nothing to do with the ministry. Thirty-eight years as a Jesuit evangelist in India had taught him one thing: He was an absolute failure.

Father Juricich did not know for what purpose the good Lord had led him to India, but he was certain that, whatever it was, it had nothing to do with saving souls.

• • •

Francis Xavier Juricich was the seventh son of a Polish coal miner, as was his father (though his mother traced her roots back to Scottish immigrants residing in Poland during the 1880's). He got his broad shoulders, thick neck, and round head from his father; his red hair and hot temper from his mother. He might have tunneled happily under Poland his whole life had it not been for the rise of Nazi Germany.

His mother had hoped from the beginning that Francis Xavier would become a priest—as evidenced by his christening—and in 1938, with the rumor of war casting a pall over Poland, she sent Francis to stay "for just a little while" with distant relatives in Scotland. For a time he attended a remedial school for refugees run by the Jesuits, but as soon as he turned eighteen, he enlisted in the British Army. He was assigned to a transport battalion and drove a truck for Montgomery in North Africa, until it struck a mine and injured his spine.

He was not certain if this was bad luck or good. A bad back is nothing to hope for, but it secured him a medal and an honorable discharge, and British citizenship by virtue of his war-wounds. It also dimmed considerably his long-term prospects for future employment, and with the resulting pain and anxiety came the insomnia that would plague Francis Xavier for the rest of his life.

He recuperated for four months at an Army hospital in Alexandria, Egypt. He sailed for England in the fall, but the ship was torpedoed off the coast of Ireland. More than five hundred men drowned that night. Seventeen survived.

Francis Xavier took his discharge in Ireland and applied for a number of odd jobs, but the condition of his back made him unfit for manual labor, even driving, and his poor English made him unsuitable for clerical work. He fumbled along from job to job, able to make do primarily because of the manpower shortage, but his luck ran out when the war ended and the troops came home.

In the summer of 1947, he applied reluctantly to enter the Jesuit Order.

He was interviewed twice by priests and examined three times by physicians. At one of the meetings, a priest asked Francis how strong his faith was. Francis replied that he believed in God but found the issue of faith and calling confusing. The truth was, he didn't really know. He left the interview dejected and was surprised two weeks later to receive a letter advising him that he had been admitted as a Novice.

Francis entered the seminary, though he felt somewhat like Jonah, vomited onto the shore from which he had fled.

Rahul Nair was nearly eighty, a staunch Malayalam Nationalist and a Hindu, well-respected in the community for both his business acumen and his charitable works. He was one of the first to invite Father Juricich into his home when Father Juricich arrived in India in 1965. They were not close but had kept up a cordial relationship.

The Nair family, more than sixty in all not counting servants, lived in a large, walled compound on the eastern side of the highway, beyond the commercial district and the railroad tracks. Father Juricich's nightly ministry sometimes took him past the Nair home. It was more impressive in the dark. Daylight revealed the urine-stained outer walls (once painted white); the crumbling stucco of the building façade; the neglected grounds; the blue plastic tarps stretched, tied, and weighted down with stones to cover the leaking roof; and the accumulation of junk bricks, cars, and spare parts strewn along the side of the house.

The Nairs had bought the compound in 1947 from a British government official, who was pulling out in anticipation of Indian independence. They had done nothing with the place since then.

This was also the year when Father Juricich passed from being a Novice to a Formed Scholastic, though Father Juricich remembered it more as the year a young Red Cross volunteer had come to his door and told him flatly that all of his Polish family had died in concentration camps—the price, the volunteer sympathized, of loyal resistance.

The wrought iron gate at the main entry stood open. The driveway was crammed with cars and motorcycles. The boys hurried Father Juricich through the front door. Inside, a number of grim-faced Nair men clutched cups of *chai*, as they occupied every available chair in the parlor, then spilled out into the hallway, where they leaned against the walls in tight-lipped silence. Candles were lighted on every table and shelf in sight.

The boys left Father Juricich in the entry. Several of the Nairs nodded, but none addressed him. A moment later, the boys returned with Naresh Nair, Rahul's oldest son. He led Father Juricich upstairs to the master bedroom.

Rahul lay in bed, attended by his wife and sisters. Dr. Bondre, a well-known local Ayurvedic physician, was concluding an examination. The family had set up a table with a statue of Shiva in one corner of the room. The image was garlanded with yellow flowers and surrounded by small candles. A stick of incense filled the room with its smoky fragrance, both salty and sweet. Dr. Bondre sorted out a container of pills with Mrs. Nair and left several bottles of oil on the dresser by the bed.

It was clear to Father Juricich what the trouble was. The old man was dressed in plain white pajamas. His arms were folded on his stomach, the covers pulled up to his chest. His white hair and flowing moustache had been combed. His right eye was closed, and a single spot of moisture glistened between the lids. Rahul had suffered a stroke.

The right side of Rahul's face sagged, his lips and chin hanging slack, but his left eye was open wide, and Rahul watched Father

Juricich alertly. With his left hand Rahul gestured for Father Juricich to come closer. Father Juricich bent his ear to Rahul, who whispered, "Priest, make me a miracle."

Father Juricich squirmed. He wasn't sure what to make of Rahul's request.

He locked eyes with Naresh, standing on the other side of the bed. Naresh was dark-complected with obsidian eyes and a thick black moustache. Despite the fact that he was over fifty, he was still a formidable man, nearly six feet tall and muscular. He was the Kannur District Secretary for the CPM, the Communist Party of Kerala, and he frequently made religion—any religion—an object of scorn in his speeches.

Mr. Nair's sisters huddled with Mrs. Nair against the far wall. They were Hindus. Mrs. Nair had once made a barefoot pilgrimage to the top of a snow-covered mountain to prove her devotion. They had shown Father Juricich pictures of the trek, but that had been a long time ago. Even then, when she was nearing forty, she had been beautiful; beautiful in the way of Indian women who eat well, practice yoga, and dress in fine silk *saris*.

It was hard, Father Juricich thought, to be a woman in India, a woman raised from infancy to be given away, often with a bribe-like dowry as an incentive for the groom's family to accept her. Once given away, she drifted like Ruth following Naomi into the house of strangers.

In this home, however, Mrs. Nair reigned supreme, a rare triumph and one deserving of respect. She had raised three sons and two daughters, and buried one of each. One daughter died of Typhoid at seventeen. One son was burned alive by anti-CPM activists who mistook him for his father. One daughter was married to an official of the Southern Railways and made her home in

Trivandrum. The other son was a dentist who had left India many years ago to live in Minnesota.

• • •

Father Juricich thought he was the least likely priest on earth to perform a miracle. Privately he wasn't sure he still believed in God, not in the proper Catholic sense of the word. He had believed for a time, after he joined the seminary, but during the eleven years between his acceptance as a Formed Scholastic and his ordination as a Professed Jesuit, through time spent in study, meditation, and practical ministry, Father Juricich had become enamored of a curiously Buddhist point in Jesuit doctrine. This initially small crack had widened into a yawning maw, which Father Juricich found increasingly difficult to straddle.

The point was this—that the truth of all faith was Love, inspired by Wisdom, interpreted in the Spirit of Charity.

Although there was an ultimate authority, the General of the Order, who resided in Rome and answered to the Pope, there was a great deal of room for interpretation within the order, so that despite its roots in the Crusades, the Jesuits today could yield activists in a variety of flavors, from revolutionary priests in Mexico, South America, Africa, and Ireland, to peace activists in Asia and the United States. Father Juricich had worked with members of both factions and found it difficult to envision them as operating under the same vow and in the same cloth.

The Jesuits themselves had no problem with this dichotomy, and since once a priest always a priest, one could run afoul of doctrine and be expelled but know he would taken back again if he asked. This Father Juricich knew all-to-well.

Once he had undertaken his own mission, he began to understand better how local conditions gradually influenced the ministry. For example, Father Juricich had long ago abandoned traditional priestly garb for a simple black *kurta* worn over pajama pants. He supposed that Rome would be appalled if they knew, but then again, they might not. In the end, it came down to practical concerns: The local clothes were cheap, comfortable, and cool in the heat, and wearing them made him more acceptable to the locals than he would have been had he persisted in Western dress.

Among Father Juricich's friends was Daniel Patrick Berrigan.

As a young man, Father Juricich had fallen under the spell of Berrigan's passionate oratory. His philosophy was a variation on the ideology of liberation theology, "Faith without works is dead." And also, "You shall know the truth, and the truth shall set you free." What good was it to pray for one's well-being if one were not willing to act—even die—to advance that well-being? What good did it do to offer sacrament to people who were little more than sheep or slaves? Wasn't it freedom of choice that distinguished humankind from the baser creatures? Revisionists like Berrigan interpreted the saints as political activists, martyred for their cause.

The ideology had made sense to Father Juricich, at least when he was younger. After all, he'd come from Poland, a country betrayed by its allies, divided and conquered, its resistance crushed, and his family had gone up the chimneys.

It took Father Juricich thirteen arduous years to become a Professed Jesuit. It took him less than two years to land before a defrocking inquest. There had been a scandal, and he had been at the center of it. Retribution was swift and sure. In the spirit of Jesuit liberality, Father Juricich was asked to take a year of reflection to decide what he wanted to do. He went to Poland, but there was nothing left of his home, so he traveled to Jerusalem with the thought that following in the Lord's footsteps might lead him to a clear understanding. He studied the lives of the early apostles, especially Thomas and Francis Xavier. Francis Xavier of the miraculous body—Father Juricich's namesake—was the first to bring the Christian ministry to India. Although he had died in China, he was buried in Goa. This period of reflection led Father Juricich to India.

It was the miracle of St. Francis Xavier that interested Father Juricich most. When Saint Francis Xavier died, to keep his body from being preserved as a relic, a servant poured four bags of lime into the coffin. Several months later, when they checked on the condition of the body, they found it entirely un-decomposed. This was in 1552. His body was transported to Goa—no small feat considering the ships of the day—and there Saint Francis Xavier was permanently interred.

In 1556 the church had dispatched a team of clerics to investigate. They'd found that the body was "incorruptible" and recommended canonization. Francis Xavier was canonized in 1622. Theoretically, Francis Xavier's body has resisted decomposition down to this day—theoretically only because in 1614 Christians from China lopped off St. Francis' right arm and took it back to China. Subsequent relic seekers removed other portions of St. Francis' anatomy, including many of his vital organs.

Father Juricich found it disconcerting that the saint could withstand corruption at the hands of nature, but was powerless to defend himself against the machinations of the church, but so it was.

Father Juricich requested that he be assigned to the archdiocese in Goa, though his arrival was met with disinterest, and he was quietly dispatched to a parish far to the south, in the lonely and neglected town of Cannanore. At first he didn't mind. Father Juricich relished the opportunity to renew his faith, and he rolled up his sleeves and went to work.

He quickly learned, however, that India had been getting on quite nicely without his interference for seven thousand years and might continue another seven thousand years without noticing he had even been there. The town itself, though it had a priest and a good number of Roman Catholic families, was predominately Orthodox Syrian Catholic. Although they welcomed the opportunity Father Juricich represented to attract Western charity to Cannanore, they had no use for him besides this. If he'd had any illusions about bringing light to the heathens, those hopes died a quick and painless death.

So far as Father Juricich knew, in thirty-eight years of service, he had not saved a single soul. Now, he stood at Rahul Nair's deathbed, and Rahul Nair was asking him for a miracle.

Father Juricich leaned forward and grasped Rahul's hand. The priest's hearing was failing with age, and Rahul's broken English, spoken with a thick Malayalam accent, had been almost impossible for him to understand, even before the stroke had slurred Rahul's speech. "What was that again?" Father Juricich asked.

"He is asking you for a miracle," Naresh said, and the old man nodded.

Father Juricich patted the old man's hands consolingly. "Miracles," he said, "happen by the grace of God. One can ask, but it is more important that one accept in one's heart that God's will, however mysterious, must be obeyed."

Obeyed, Father Juricich thought. One could almost examine life more accurately through the long list of commandments not obeyed. There was that one original commandment about the fruit of the tree of the knowledge of good and evil, which was not to be eaten. From the beginning it was decided that man should not decide, yet what was man but a patchwork of nerves, instincts, and impulses, constantly at cross-purposes with the spiritual instructions. For example, consider, "Thou shalt not covet thy neighbor's wife."

From the first command came the Ten Commandments, and from the ten arose a host of proscribed laws governing every conceivable human behavior. From these laws came the Son of Man saying, "Love is the Law's fulfillment," and now there was something higher than law but less specific, more open to interpretation, and it seemed to Father Juricich that the older he got, the less he was certain about anything.

Rahul mumbled something Father Juricich could not hear. He looked at Naresh, who said, "He wants you to take him to visit my brother in America."

Father Juricich almost fell out of his chair. "He wants what?"

• • •

At home, Father Juricich found Shunita busy in the kitchen.

When he came in, she turned without speaking and pulled a chair back from the table.

He sat down—he had long ago given up arguing with Shunita about domestic matters—and she poured him a cup of coffee, then served him rice and vegetable *korma* with a small bowl of fish curry on the side and some fresh *iddly* to blot up the gravy. He ate with his fingers, then washed his hands and retired to his room to think.

When it was dark, Father Juricich came back into the kitchen. Shunita was curled up, asleep on a mat in the corner, but she had left coffee in a pan on the stove. He warmed it and drank, feeling the whole time that she was awake and watching him. When he had finished, he took his walking stick and set out on his nightly rounds.

It had taken Father Juricich years to find his calling (if he truly had a calling). The walking had begun with the doubts that gnawed at his faith and manifested themselves in chronic insomnia.

Upon Father Juricich's arrival, there had been six hundred Catholic families in Cannanore, all of whom could trace their practice back practically to the Portuguese colonization. He had served in Cannanore for thirty-eight years, and now there were still six hundred Catholic families, the births offset by deaths, immigration to other countries, or migration to the big cities. This, in a town of a million people. The daughters married into other Catholic families, usually from out-of-town, and moved away. The sons married the daughters of other Catholic families, usually from out-of-town, and moved them into their family homes.

If one wasn't careful, one might confuse Indian Catholics with Hindus. The Indian Catholics placed objects of devotion by their front doors and images at strategic points in their houses. They decorated these images with orange flowers, burned candles and incense, and built small shrines that looked like Hindu *stupas* in their yards. Despite the Church's dire warnings about "godless Communism," most of the locals ignored the Papal edict and voted Communist, anyway.

Father Juricich gradually and grudgingly gave up the idea that he could change the locals (for better or worse).

Over time, he gave up on the notion that religion—any religion—made the slightest difference in people's lives. He wrote letters requesting transfers to other districts, maintaining that he was ineffective in Cannanore, and even threatened to quit the priesthood, all for naught. No replacement was forthcoming.

Then, the insomnia had set in, and to cure the insomnia, his nightly walks.

Tonight, he was passing through the main bazaar around two o'clock in the morning when he came across two men cleaning out sewer pipes. They raked through the muck with their bare hands, looking for coins or whatever else of value might turn up.

It was an especially dark night, and Father Juricich watched the two men with a kind of morbid fascination. The *monsoons* were ending, a strong sea breeze was blowing, and a thinning canopy of clouds raced overhead. Suddenly, the moon burst through the clouds, and Father Juricich saw that the man closest to him was horribly deformed—his skin from head to toe a massive eruption of what looked like beads, clustered together so tightly that he barely looked human. His companion, too, was deformed, but in a different way. Leprosy had eaten away most of his hands, feet, nose, lips, and ears. As soon as they saw Father Juricich, they shrank back, but Father Juricich raised his hands and said in broken Malayalam, "Wait."

He carried a small backpack with a bottle of water and a light meal he had intended to eat later on. Instead, he offered the food to the men. They shook their heads, but eventually Father Juricich persuaded them.

Afterward, Father Juricich produced two oranges from his bag, peeled them, and insisted that the two men eat these also.

He asked them their names.

Thennala and Kandoth were their names, they said. Their stories were identical. They came from poor villages in the mountains, and had both been stricken as children. Their families could not afford to care for them, so the boys came to city to beg, but as their diseases had progressed, they had become so ugly that they could not survive—even by begging. So, they had begun to sleep days and prowl nights, eking out a living on what they could scavenge from garbage piles and sewer lines.

"Where do you sleep," Father Juricich asked.

They led him through the bazaar to a slot between two old buildings, where a gap less than a foot wide formed a narrow alley.

Father Juricich squeezed into the space and followed them down the side and around the rear of one building to a closet-sized open space, where they had built a tent of plastic sheeting over a narrow platform, upon which they shared a single filthy mattress. The owner of the building, Thennala explained, allowed them to stay there in exchange for their picking up the trash and sweeping the sidewalk in front of the building.

Sitting on the mattress was a small, malnourished boy, dressed only in underpants and staring into space. Kandoth had saved half of his orange, and he placed it in the boy's hand. The boy did not acknowledge him, but after holding the orange for a moment, he ate it.

In the dim light, Father Juricich saw Kandoth kneeling in front of the boy. If Kandoth had had lips, Father Juricich thought they would have been parted in a tender smile.

"He is mute," Thennala said. "Like an animal."

This was how it began.

The following night, Father Juricich took rice and *iddly* left over from his own dinner to Thennala, Kandoth, and the boy. He came again a few nights later, bringing clothes and sandals.

After a week of regular visits, Thennala told the priest about another homeless man, a legless beggar who lived in a culvert under the highway. And then there were two children who turned up, orphans apparently, one perhaps five and the other two. The younger boy's legs were backwards from birth; he would never walk. And then they came out of the woodwork—the lepers, the crippled, the blind, the sick, the lame, the insane.

Within six months, Father Juricich was making regular rounds, dispensing food, medicine, clothing, tarps, and bedding, sometimes talking, sometimes listening. He visited ruined buildings and culverts under the railroad tracks. He found bridges, patches of woods, and caves hollowed out by the sea. He learned his way through the maze of drainage ditches, the open sewers that carried away the runoff from the *monsoon* and the waste from the houses, to find the hidden spots where the deformed passed their nights— or days—undisturbed.

They slipped into town in the middle of the night and ate from garbage cans in the alleys behind restaurants or wrenched spoiled fish from stray cats in the city market. Some were outwardly deformed, limbs withered from disease or missing from birth. They were syphilitic. They were blind from herpes. They had been burned and mutilated. And there were others, too, like the boy—not outwardly damaged, but speechless, or psychotic, or schizophrenic.

For ten years Father Juricich had lived in Cannanore, and he had never seen any of these people. In six months he knew more than a hundred by name.

At first, he fed them from his own kitchen, or rather, a grumbling Shunita fed them. She cooked, and Father Juricich made the rounds. When there were more to feed than Father Juricich could reach in a night, Thennala and Kandoth began helping him.

He wrote to the archdiocese in Goa and requested money for a kitchen and a car, but they replied that he would have to find funds from the local community. He approached the local Church committee but was rebuffed.

He tried the Communist party office and presented his case as a cause for equality. They listened to his overture sympathetically. Party workers were dispatched to local unions with letters asking for donations, and Father Juricich received some clothes and sandals, a pittance of rice from the rice-growers cooperative, and a small allowance of fish from the fisherman's cooperative.

Over time, however, an ideological split developed in the party, and many members came to resent a supposedly Western institution begging off them.

"Who are these people?" they asked, meaning the deformed. "Let them approach us directly." A committee was set up to care for the homeless. It fizzled in less than a year.

Around that time, Thennala and Kandoth led Father Juricich to the edge of town, where he found the most hideous human being he had yet met—a woman, perhaps thirty years old, emaciated from malnutrition and shivering from malaria, crouched in a railway culvert. The true extent of her deformity was almost beyond description, for the whole right side of her face was swollen into a ghastly, demonic apparition. Her nose extended nearly a foot, a protuberance that looked more like the trunk of a young elephant than anything human. She was hunchbacked, and her right arm had been broken and healed unset, so that it was no longer functional.

She huddled against the wall, wearing the remains of a burlap sack fashioned into a crude dress.

"How long has she been like this?" Father Juricich asked.

Thennala shrugged his shoulders. "We only heard about her last night. Some children saw her and thought she was dead."

"She will be if we don't get her to a hospital."

Father Juricich reached for the woman, but she recoiled and hissed at him like a snake. "Tell her that I won't hurt her," he said.

Thennala said something in Malayalam, but the woman did not respond. Kandoth tried some broken Hindi, but the woman gave no sign of recognition. Eventually, Kandoth was dispatched to the Syrian-Christian hospital to fetch an ambulance, and it arrived near dawn. The woman was wrestled down, strapped to a stretcher, and carted away, howling like a dog.

The following afternoon Father Juricich visited her. The staff had placed her in a private ward, because they knew the other patients would riot rather than share a room with her. She was heavily sedated.

"Has anyone spoken to her?" he asked.

The nurse replied that they had tried a half-dozen languages, but she had responded to none of them.

For two weeks, Father Juricich visited the woman every afternoon, bringing her bits of banana, pineapple, and milk *peda* to supplement her hospital diet. She gained weight and strength. Antibiotics checked the malaria. Even so, day after day, when Father Juricich visited, he found the woman with her face to the wall.

He wrote letters inquiring about missing women to state officials. They replied that there were thousands of missing women in India and no official means of keeping track of them. In fact, no one wanted to keep track of them. It was hard enough to place healthy, beautiful girls with husbands, without having to worry about the crazy or deformed. They were sorry to hear about her troubles. She was lucky someone hadn't burned or drowned her.

Father Juricich got his temper up over this, and he began writing letters, not just to the archdiocese in Goa, but back to Rome. He wrote international women's organizations, the United Nations, and the Dalai Lama. He wrote the American President, Jimmy Carter, thinking surely he would listen.

One morning a Tibetan monk called at his door. He had read about the priest who worked with deformed beggars in Kerala and had traveled from Kathmandu to meet him. Father Juricich was stunned. He wasn't aware that anyone had taken note of his work, but the monk produced an article clipped from the *Kathmandu Times* about Father Juricich and his letter-writing campaign. The monk asked Father Juricich if he could accompany him that night as he made his rounds. Together, they visited the culvert where the "elephant woman"—finally discharged from the hospital—now made her home.

The woman kept a small pile of cow dung smoldering, not that it was cold, but because the smoke kept the mosquitoes at bay. The priest offered her *biryani* wrapped in a torn page of newspaper.

She squatted on her haunches and ate with her fingers.

The monk squatted down opposite her and waited. When she had finished eating, he said something in Tibetan. She froze. He repeated the phrase, and her eyes widened. The monk smiled, asked a question, and the woman nodded, then burst into tears. She fell to the ground, curled up into a ball, covered her face, and rolled away from them. Father Juricich held her until she stopped sobbing.

After she had composed herself, the monk squatted beside her, and they talked.

This was her story. She had likely been born in Tibet and taken to Nepal when she was an infant. She remembered a room in a city, perhaps Kathmandu, with other families who had children. They slept in the same room, huddled together to stay warm. Later on, they'd moved, probably to India. She described another city. It was hot. She remembered mosquitoes. It might have been Mumbai, but it might have been Calcutta, or Delhi, as they each have colonies of Tibetan refugees.

She had been diseased from infancy. Her mother cared for her but kept her swathed in blankets to hide her face. She remembered her father but not the reason he'd left the family.

The monk suggested it might have been to work, for Tibetan men often sought work overseas.

Apparently he never came back.

The mother took the child on a journey by train. The girl was too young to know where they were going, but it must have been somewhere north, for she remembered it was cold. The mother took sick and died, suddenly, there on the train.

She remembered that there was a commotion, people shouting. She was frightened. She wandered away, unnoticed in the crowd, and got off the train, she didn't know where.

She lived for a while in a rail yard, sleeping in empty boxcars. A man used to share his food with her. She looked forward to his company, for he was kind.

She must have been ten or eleven when a gang of teenage boys came along one night and raped her. They made her keep a blanket wrapped around her face while they did it. When they were finished, they wrapped her in the blanket and took her away in the trunk of a car. They stopped, took her out, and then she was falling. They'd thrown her off a bridge into a river. She hit the abutment and fractured her arm—that was how it came to be useless.

How long ago was this? She shrugged her shoulders. Who knows? She'd crawled out of the river and remained hidden in the woods, until hunger and pain drove her out.

In a small village, she was taken to a doctor. He immobilized her arm without setting the bone, and then he gave her some pills to fight infection. In another day or so, the clinic turned her out onto the streets, and she began following the railroad tracks south, living off of the garbage which people threw from the train.

Years passed. She spoke to no one. One day, she'd come to this place, when she was very sick. Now, she called it home.

The monk asked if she had a name.

The woman shook her head.

Was there something she wanted to be called?

No response.

Father Juricich patted the woman gently on the shoulder. "I shall call you Sofia," he said, "after my mother."

The following morning, the monk left. He promised to take up the priest's cause. Six months passed, and Father Juricich heard nothing.

This, Father Juricich reflected, was not a success that inspired faith. Taking a deep breath, he drew upon a lesson he had learned as a disciple of Father Berrigan: "Make yourself the crossroads where your enemies collide."

He continued to write letters. He wrote a letter to the local Communist party and accused them of showing no more compassion than the Western capitalist dogs. He wrote a letter to the Secretary of State of the United States, saying that the Communists were winning in India because other countries stood by and did nothing to alleviate the suffering of the masses. He wrote a letter to the Pope, claiming that his neglect was driving the flock into the hands of the Communists or the fold of the Muslims. He wrote to the United Nations and accused them of practicing "pretty" charity, offering aid where photos of beautiful children exuding charm and gratitude could be used to make the bureaucracy look good, while neglecting those most desperately in need.

The first delegation to arrive was from the local Communist party, headed by Naresh Nair. He had asked, with obvious distaste, what they could do.

"I want you to organize the deformed into their own cooperative. They provide you with a valuable service. You will provide them with the means to support themselves with dignity."

The members of the delegation looked at each other and scratched their heads. "What service do these beggars perform?" Naresh asked.

Father Juricich had acquired the Indian habit of talking with his hands, and he gestured emphatically at every point. "They pick up your garbage and unclog your sewers. They perform the most necessary and menial tasks of decent civilization, and you have not the compassion even to feed or clothe them properly. Put out garbage cans, and let them clean the streets at night. Give them tools and brooms, so that they can work efficiently. Give them a wage, or at least, let them eat the leftovers from your restaurants. Find someone to make them decent clothes. They might be deformed, but they don't have to be indecent."

The cooperative was formed, and most of Father Juricich's demands were met.

The Nair family was, in Indian terms, prosperous. They owned several restaurants, a small tourist hotel, a printing business, and a dozen or so three-wheel auto-rickshaws that they hired out to cabbies for a daily fee.

Rahul in particular seemed amused by Father Juricich's request for aid, but being a practical man, he took the lead and pressed the local Lion's and Rotary Clubs to support the priest. Following his lead, many local restaurants began to leave their leftovers in crates behind the back doors. In return, they found their sidewalks swept and windows washed in the morning.

Nair himself hired several of the deformed to work nights. One cleaned his auto rickshaws. Another, he taught to operate the printing press after hours, when he had rush orders.

A few months later, a delegation arrived from New Delhi and asked what they could do for the "hidden homeless" on a national scale. Two officials were assigned to follow Father Juricich around for a week and calculate what percentage of the local population might be homeless and in need, yet not registered with the census.

They left, and few months later, Father Juricich received a letter advising him that one of the local hospitals had budgeted a small amount to care for the mentally ill.

A similar letter arrived from the United Nations. They would send a team to study Father Juricich's ministry and see what could be learned, so that these people could be helped on an international scale.

The representatives spent a week in Cannanore, then departed.

A few months later, the United Nations proposed, through the World Health Organization, to initiate a grassroots campaign to identify and provide basic services for the poorest of the poor. They cited Mother Teresa as a role model.

The United States ear-marked money for the relief of the poor as well, though these funds were pillaged so thoroughly by corrupt officials at the national and state levels that, as far as Father Juricich could tell, not a dime ever made it to the needy.

Finally, Father Juricich received a letter advising him that a delegation from Rome would be dispatched to see him, and for the first time in his career as a priest, he was proud.

The local families banded together to paint the church and prepare a welcome feast. They served spiced fish, steamed in banana leaves, with saffron rice and vegetable *masala*. The delegates smiled, led Mass, offered special prayers, and made glowing pronouncements about the little community that could. Afterwards, in private, they warned Father Juricich that he had been sent to Cannanore as a punishment, and said that if he knew what was good for him, he would keep a low profile. There were still those who did not like to be reminded of his presence.

When they left, he sank into a deep depression.

• • •

Twenty years passed. Father Juricich, walking in the dark, stepped into a hole and fell. He broke his right leg so badly that he could not extract himself, so he lay in the middle of the road until workers found him in the morning. His first recollection was being lifted by many hands and gently placed on a stretcher.

Surgeons from the Orthodox-Syrian hospital set the bone. They gave him a private room for his recovery. After that, he took to walking with a cane, not so much because he needed it to stand, but because, like a blind man, he could feel the road ahead of his every step.

As Father Juricich approached his eightieth birthday, his nightly rounds felt more like visiting old friends. He no longer needed to distribute meals, though he carried a pocketful of milk *peda* candies to share with homeless children. He also dispensed antibiotics and other medicines as needed, to those still reluctant to come into town for assistance.

Thennala and Sofia remained his closest friends. Kandoth had died some years back, but Thennala still plugged on, living squeezed like a cockroach inro the same crack between the same buildings. He had, for a time, been elected a representative to the state government under the rules requiring representation by the lower castes, but had found politics difficult and felt that the public display of his handicap actually worked against the needs of the poor.

Sofia had moved closer to town and lived a squatter's hut she had built on the fenced grounds surrounding an electrical transformer. She had learned enough Malayalam to get by, and often came to visit Father Juricich, arriving at his home in the late afternoon when she knew he would be getting ready for his rounds. She still swathed her face in a shawl, and in the dark she almost passed for a Muslim, with only her eyes and nose visible through the veil.

• • •

Father Juricich slept fitfully, waking every few hours from dreams that were sometimes rhapsodic, and at other times disturbingly sexual.

He woke shortly before noon, performed his devotional, eeked out a sparse breakfast under Shunita's critical eye, and set out to check on Rahul Nair.

The Nair compound was slightly less crowded, though a number of relatives still camped out downstairs and in the hall. Upstairs, Mrs. Nair, looking pale, sat on the edge of the bed. She stood and stepped to one side when Father Juricich arrived. The old man looked as if he hadn't moved since the previous visit.

"Tell me," Father Juricich said, pulling a chair close to the bed, "why do you want to go to America?"

Rahul spoke slowly, laboriously churning out the words. "I want to visit my son."

"Why do you want me to take you?"

"I have no money."

"What do you mean? You are one of the wealthiest men in town."

"This is not so. I have divided a little for all of my sons and grandsons, but for myself, there is nothing. I will die soon. I must visit my son."

"But the Nair fortune…"

"There is no fortune. We have been living on reputation. What I had was sufficient for myself, but divided among my sons—"

The priest rested his elbow on his knee and his chin in his hand. "But your son in America—"

"He has supported us with a portion of his income for years. It was his duty to the family, but he and I have had an ongoing disagreement from many years ago. He will not come here. He will not send for me. I must go to him. It is the only way."

"What happened between you and your son?"

"There are two things, priest," Rahul said. "If I tell you, you must repeat them to no one. It must be as though we never spoke."

"All right."

"First, many years ago, I suspected my wife of adultery. This was probably a foolish jealousy on my part, but something may also have happened. Over the years, I paused to question whether or not Venkadath was really mine. I favored Naresh, though Venkadath's mother favored him. Perhaps this division forced him to leave. He wanted to go to America. I did not care if he stayed, but then when he married an American girl, a Christian, and when he became a Christian himself, I told him that he was no longer my son, if he ever was—"

"And now?"

"We are old, priest, and many things change. A young man sees everything and knows nothing, because he has no perspective from which to understand. An old man sees nothing and knows everything, because everything he sees reminds him of something else that was. I know much now that I did not see then. Have you read Khalil Gibran?"

"Yes."

"Then you know that children may be given us, but that they are never really ours. I failed my son, and now I want only to give him back the thing I took from him, the respect of his father. He will not come to me, priest. I must go to him. I am poor, but I am no longer too proud to ask for help. I have no time for the luxury of pride. You will help me, yes?"

"Rahul, I would do anything to help you, but I have taken a vow of poverty regarding the things of this world. I have only a small pension from the church, a home, and a few pieces of clothing. What would you have me do?"

"With all of the power at your command, is there no one you can write? No authority you can draw on?"

"It would take a miracle for me to find enough money to send you to America, and you are not well. How would you withstand the rigors of the journey?"

"For how many years you have told us, 'With God, anything is possible.' Now you say that it will take a miracle? Show me the miracle. I can make the journey priest. If you can provide the money, I will join your church."

Father Juricich limped home, his leg aching for no apparent reason. In Europe, people claimed that aching bones meant a change in the weather. In Kerala, there were two summers and two *monsoons*—not much change to ache over.

At home, Shunita had marinated a chicken and roasted it on a skewer—one of Father Juricich's favorite dishes. With the chicken, she served rice and vegetables, steamed together with bay leaves and cloves in a banana leaf. Sofia was there, too, sitting in a corner when he arrived.

Father Juricich paused only to wash his face and hands, then joined them in the kitchen. He picked at his food. Lately, even his favorite meals did not rouse his interest.

Shunita scolded him for not eating. She made him lime tea.

Sofia went out and returned an hour later with Thennala. He brought some cake. "The bakery left it for me," he explained.

"I'm just tired," Father Juricich said. "I haven't been sleeping well."

"What is happening with old man Nair?" Thennala asked.

"It is quite absurd, really. He wants me to send him to America."

"To America? Why? Are there not doctors enough here?"

"It is about his son, not his condition."

"His son is also a doctor?"

"A dentist, but that is not the reason. I really can't say any more about it. I promised."

"Why would he ask you?"

"He thinks that I can help, the foolish old man." Father Juricich grimaced and rubbed his forehead with his right hand. "He says he'll convert to Christianity, if I can send him to America."

"Convert? You must be joking."

"I would never joke about a think like that."

• • •

That night, lying in bed, Father Juricich pondered the intricacies of Indian familial life. Men could have—or used to have—second wives, though the laws had changed about that, recently. Now, they often had girlfriends, whom they kept with the full knowledge of their wives. Wives might not approve of the arrangement, but there was little that they could do about it.

Once divorced, Indian women almost never remarried. They might be kept in their birth home, but they might also be thrown out into the streets to fend for themselves.

On the other hand, women caught at adultery could be stoned or even burned alive. The double standard was perplexing, but not entirely unlike Western culture.

Who knew what the future held? Father Juricich was seventy-nine years old, and no mention had been made of his retiring, no replacement groomed or even thought of, as far as he knew.

When he had first arrived in Cannanore, Father Juricich suggested that the Church host traditional morning Masses at six o'clock, ten o'clock, and noon. The local priest told him to go ahead if he wanted to. What Father Juricich found was that, in Kerala, people didn't stir from their homes until ten. They spent the cool morning hours sleeping or tending to domestic affairs. The six o'clock Mass failed during the first week, for not a single parishioner showed. He canceled the ten o'clock within a month, and the noon by the end of his first year.

The flock had met once a week on Sundays, probably since St. Francis himself had preached to them. One energetic priest was not going to turn the tide of five hundred years of tradition, and if Father Juricich couldn't affect even a small flock of supposedly faithful followers, what chance did he have to work a miracle for a non-believer? By what right did he even ask?

Rahul was partly right, Father Juricich thought. A young man saw everything and knew nothing. An old man saw nothing and knew...nothing?

That night, instead of making his usual rounds, Father Juricich rested in his room. He fell asleep during the early hours of the morning and dreamed of Tunisia. Upon waking, he recalled the dream, seeing General Montgomery pass by in his staff car early one morning. The general was resplendent, wearing a crisp uniform with a black scarf and a red beret.

Then-Corporal Juricich saluted, and the general acknowledged the salute by waving his riding crop.

Awakening in his room, Father Juricich remembered the seemingly endless moment of paralytic fear, when his truck had struck the mine. He had felt himself lifted up and thrown (as he later described it) "ass over teakettle."

He remembered the shock of the troop ship's being struck by the torpedo. Father Juricich had been on deck late—another of his insomniac nights, and the force of the explosion had hurled him into the water. His first fear had been that he had re-injured his back, but though he felt the grate of bone on bone, he could still swim well enough to stay afloat until a rescue ship caught him in its spotlight.

Still, for a few terrifying moments, he had been utterly alone in the waters of the North Atlantic, and it had been cold, and he had wondered about his family, and whether his mother had really done him a favor by whisking him out of Poland, ahead of the invasion.

Nothing he had experienced since that moment, alone in the North Atlantic, had challenged his realization that a man is insignificant compared to the universe.

Even so, in that moment, floating numb in the freezing water, Father Juricich knew with certainty that he was not going to die, and that having dodged death's hammer-stroke twice, God must have something greater in store for him. That was the spark of faith that had kept him going.

Now, sixty years later, Father Francis Xavier Juricich could not say what that greater thing was, and for the first time in years, he wept.

In the early afternoon, he emerged from his room, ashen and refusing anything but tea. He retired to the church, where he prayed alone and fell asleep in the front pew.

Thennala woke him, gently shaking the priest's shoulder.

"How much," he asked, "is a ticket to America?"

Father Juricich was confused. "What," he replied. "Is everyone going to America, now?"

"No, I only wondered."

"I don't know, but it must be many *lakhs* of *rupees*. Ask Suliman, the travel agent. He would know."

That evening Father Juricich felt somewhat refreshed. He ate more than he had in several days, but afterwards his stomach cramped, and he took to bed.

In the morning, Shunita summoned a doctor.

The doctor listened to Father Juricich's rumbling bowels through a cold stethoscope and then prescribed a combination of antibiotics and Ayurvedic medication.

Thennala came to visit during the afternoon, and Sofia in the evening.

The following day was Sunday. Father Juricich was well enough to lead Mass, though he shortened his sermon to a few words, citing his poor health as an excuse.

No one complained.

After the service, he was met outside by Thennala, who asked Father Juricich how much money he could contribute towards a ticket for Rahul Nair. Thennala had inquired of the travel agent and also the physician, who said it was impossible for Rahul to travel alone, and that if he were to make the trip at all, a nurse would have to be in constant attendance.

"Are you gone mad?" Father Juricich asked.

Thennala shook his head.

Father Juricich had set aside a small portion of his pension for emergencies. "I suppose," he said, "if it came down to it, I could contribute five or ten thousand rupees."

Thennala burst into a radiant smile. "Then it is done," he replied.

"What?" Father Juricich gasped. "How?"

"We all chipped in," Thennala said. Every one his portion. You have done much for us. It was time we did something for you."

Rahul Nair and his nurse left for Minneapolis on a Thursday morning, with a large delegation turning out at the bus terminal to see them off. Father Juricich, though still bothered by his stomach, turned out also, leaning heavily on his staff.

Afterward, and for the first time in weeks, he slept soundly, undisturbed by dreams. He awoke around three, dined with Shunita, and left near seven for his nightly rounds.

Thennala found him the next morning unconscious by the side of the road. On his eightieth birthday, Father Juricich had been struck by a car.

Ruhal Nair suffered another stroke on the plane on the way home from America and died 36,000 feet over the Pacific Ocean. Father Juricich received the news stoically, lying in his hospital bed. Unless there was some private pact between Rahul and God, it seemed Father Juricich would die with his perfect record of evangelistic ineptitude intact. Perhaps, he wondered, they will name an order after me, someday. The Juricichians—dedicated to burying their heads in the sand and converting no one. It would be an easy order to belong to. Or would it?

That night Father Juricich dreamed of Poland, and of the long train ride that had carried him to France, and then of the ship that had taken him to Scotland, and of the distant relatives who had met him on the pier when he arrived. The dream was confusing, for Scotland was hot and covered with palm trees, and the Atlantic was flat and calm, and among the relatives were dozens of friends and co-workers whom Father Juricich had known much later in life, and Father Juricich was so tired when he arrived that he could hardly walk down the gangway.

Shunita found him in the morning, when he failed to rise for his coffee. Father Juricich had died in his sleep.

By nightfall, the little cottage behind the church was awash with a sea of lighted candles. Notes arrived from Muslims and Hindus. Even the local Communist party chief placed a wreath in the front yard.

From as far away as Calcutta, the blind, the lame, the sick, and the deformed came to pay their respects—thousands upon thousands, walking in the light of day to reach Cannanore.

Father Juricich had left a will. In his own, typically headstrong fashion, he had requested that his body be cremated.

• • •

Two months later a replacement priest arrived from Goa. The new priest settled into the cottage. Shunita cooked and cleaned for him, but he made no effort, as Father Juricich had, to walk the streets at night. One morning, over coffee, he asked Shunita who had been with Father Juricich after he died, and if the whispers about him were true.

"What do they whisper?" Shunita asked.

"They say that a long time ago, when Father Juricich was in Ireland, he was involved in a scandal with a married woman, a Protestant, at that. They were found out, and someone—nobody knows who—took him and the woman away. The woman was killed, but the priest, according to rumor, was castrated. His penis was cut off, too. I just wondered if, when they washed the body, and I suppose someone must have washed the body, if anyone saw anything…unusual."

Shunita considered the question for a moment, and then refilled the priest's cup. "No," she said, shaking her head for emphasis. "He was perfect."

What she remembered about the day, however, was that when Sofia heard the news, she rushed into the cottage and threw herself onto the priest's body, and that she could be neither torn from that embrace, nor consoled.

Mark D. Hart

WYCH ELM
From the Book of Lismore

What might be the harm of it?
The old elm in the abbey
dripped a marvelous sap
in which each soul could taste
the very flavor it desired.

A Christ-like tree of mercy—
a flow from its pierced side.
St. Ruadhán, abbot of Lorrha,
let the mystery be, let
the people have earth's solace.

But it bothered the monks.
They went to St. Findian,
Ruadhán's teacher, to put
an end to this offending font.
Findian traveled to Lorrha.

He made a sign of the cross
over the tree, and it never dripped
another drop. But Ruadhán
blessed a nearby well, so it drew
that same wonderful sap.

Findian turned it back to water,
told him to stop his blessings.
Two versions of grace, two ways
to deal in a new dispensation with
the Old Orchard's lingering fruit.

Mark D. Hart

YEW

Churchyard tree,
your gnarled trunk
twists like a rope strung

between earth and heaven.
In that time of darkness
when green things sleep,

animals shiver, and humans
warm by the fire,
as clouds lower their bellies,

leaves and eaves drip,
as the soul
retreats into silence,

you, the dark yew,
evergreen, persevere.
November, Samhain

is yours, the year's end,
winter's beginning
in the old Celtic reckoning,

when extra livestock
are culled to
conserve the winter feed,

when the veil thins
between this world
and that other—to which

we also belong.

Janelle Adsit

[MERCY]

the difficult atoms
condensing
into 100 suns

our wonder
ballooned
under us

our disgrace—
the dark
frantic
singular
indication

god's mercy
we beat

blessings
win all

steel
towers
vapor

LALITAMBA

trains canceled
stricken records
no satin shining

the linger
the afterwhir

hot day falling
as cold
deep
layers

these things we can't undo

Sarah Estes

PLATO'S CAVE

Neurons bright and tentacled
thrust into the random dark.
Cellar steps narrow into sleep.

Every tentacle touches something.
Every subject becomes an object.
Every object becomes englutted,
salt-muscled and hard.

The inhaled sex of death, a sea
cucumber. Clams furrow ruddy paths
along the earth-side wall. Calcine shell
opens to celiac brain and pushes forward.

Anemone breasts bloom a white pink
in the cold briny water. On a high shelf
root potatoes sit like swallowed suns.

Who could leave this cave of edible need,
with the water rising all night
             and no way up the stairs.

Sarah Estes

ULTIMATE TELOS

To become unreachable
in the far corners of rural darkness,
where the soft-tilled edges of civilized
       fields meld to the wild.

Children who ran too far would be lost,
       evaporating into storybook
endings—caught in bear traps, eaten
by coyotes, or taken and raised
       for their own.

Games were but filaments, human
spiders letting their webs to the dark,
       tenuous tethers of the known world.

Rope slacked and rope pulled,
Night was just beginning
       to extinguish them.

 They will pick up again tomorrow.

Let us not fool ourselves.
This is where art begins.

CONTRIBUTOR NOTES

JANELL ADSIT is the author of the poetry collection *Unremitting Entrance* (Spuyten Duyvil, 2014). Her poetry, book reviews, and essays have appeared in publications such as *Confrontation*, *Caketrain*, *Mid-American Review*, *Colorado Review*, and *Foreword*.

BRUCE ALFORD'S first collection was *Terminal Switching* (Elk River Review Press, 2007). He was an assistant professor of creative writing at the University of South Alabama from 2007 until 2011. Before working in academia, he served as an inner-city missionary. The piece included is excerpted from a poem cycle entitled "Alford's Devotional and Guide to Poetry." Alford wrote the devotional to help him work through his mother's death from cancer, his father's death from West Nile virus two years earlier, and the loss of his job as a creative writing instructor. "I wanted to create a moment of grace in an otherwise painful chronicle," he states.

MARK ALI is an English teacher, program coordinator, and Bay Area Writing Project teacher consultant. He holds degrees from California State University East Bay. His work has appeared in *Digital Paper*, *Pearl*, and *Rad Dad*. Mark has attended the workshops A Thousand Words, Room to Write, and Gather, and has studied with Stephen Gutierrez and Marty Williams. He is also a member of a writing group that he has worked with since 2012. He lives in Oakland, California, with his wife and two sons.

DEVON BALWIT is a poet, parent, and educator in Portland, Oregon. Her poems have been published or are forthcoming in a variety of print and online journals, which she thanks here: *3 Elements, Birds Piled Loosely, Drylandlit, Dying Dahlia Review, Leveler, Off) Course,* the *Cape Rock,* the *Fem, Fog Machine, New Verse News, Prick of the Spindle,* the *Sow's Ear Poetry Review, Yellow Chair Review, Timberline Review, Txt Objx, Vox Poetica,* and *Vanilla Sex Magazine.*

CHRYSTAL BERCHE writes. Hard times, troubled times. The lives of her characters are never easy, but then what life is? The story is in the struggle, the journey, the triumphs, and the falls. She writes about artists, musicians, loners, drifters, dreamers, hippies, bikers, truckers, hunters, and all the other things she knows and loves. When she isn't writing, she's taking pictures or curled up with a good book and a kitty on her lap.

LAURIE KING-BILLMAN has had writings published in *13th Moon, San Pedro River Review,* the *MacGuffin,* the *Penmen Review,* the *Rambler, Ragazine, Streetlight,* the *Mom Egg,* and several anthologies. She attended the North Carolina Writer's Conference from 2004 to 2010, where she studied with Joanna Catherine Scott, Ruth Moose, and Karen Pullen. She has worked as a mental health therapist for several Native American tribes and currently works with their youth and families.

DR. EDWARD BRUCE BYNUM is a clinical psychologist and the author of several texts in psychology, including *Dark Light Consciousness* (Inner Traditions, 2012) and *The African Unconscious* (Cosimo Books, 2012). He is a recipient of the American Psychological Association's Abraham Maslow Award. He is the author of several volumes of poetry, including *Godzillananda: His Life and Visions* (Brutal Swan Press, 1996), which won the 2010 Naomi Long Madgett Poetry Prize. The present piece is excerpted from a longer unpublished work called "Confessions from the Earth." He is a *yogi* and lives near Amherst, Massachusetts.

FRANK CAVANO is a retired physician whose writings attempt to comment on the complexity of the human condition, with all its fragility, pain, *pathos*, and beauty. Many of his efforts invoke a spiritual or inspirational perspective. In the last eight years, more than 100 of his pieces have found a home online and/or in print. He is always grateful when a poem stimulates new thought or strikes an emotional chord with a reader.

BRENT DICKSON is a graduate of Middlebury College. In 1998, he retired, after spending 35 years investing money for others. Since then, he has been filling time by hiking, practicing *yoga*, painting watercolors, writing memoirs, and learning to speak Italian. He and his wife live on the coast of Massachusetts. They have two sons and four grandchildren. During his professional career, he acquired considerable creative writing experience by authoring monthly prognostications on the economy and the stock market.

SARAH ESTES' work has appeared in *Agni*, the *Atlantic*, *Christian Science Monitor*, *Cimarron*, *Crab Orchard Review*, *Field*, *New Orleans Review*, *Southern Review*, and elsewhere. She obtained an M.F.A. from the University of Virginia as a Hoynes Fellow and an M.A. Religion and Culture from Harvard University.

EYES OF FIRE is a Cree elder who beheld a vision of the future and spoke the legend of the Rainbow Warriors.

PATRICIA FAREWELL has had work published in the *Green Mountains Review*, the *American Poetry Review*, the *Partisan Review*, *Chelsea*, the *New York Quarterly*, and other magazines. Her first book won the Story Line Press Frederick Morgan Poetry Prize.

Graphic artist and painter ALLEN FORREST was born in Canada and bred in the United States. He has created cover art and illustrations for literary publications and books. He is the winner of the Leslie Jacoby Honor for Art from San Jose State University's *Reed* magazine. His Bel Red painting series is part of the Bellevue College Foundation's permanent art collection. Forrest's expressive drawing and painting style is a mix of avant-garde expressionism and post-Impressionist elements, reminiscent of Van Gogh.

MARK HART's first collection *Boy Singing to Cattle* (Pearl Editions, 2013) won the Pearl Poetry Prize and was named a Must-Read Book by the Massachusetts Center for the Book in 2014. Raised on a wheat farm in the Palouse region of eastern Washington State, he now lives in an apple orchard in western Massachusetts.

DOUG HILE has been gathering material over a lifetime and was encouraged to document some of it by Elisavietta Ritchie, through her writers' workshop. She is a source of inspiration, as are Isaac Asimov, Greg Bear, and quite a few others. Life is good in Southern Maryland.

ELIOT HUDSON is a New York based writer who earned an M.Sc. in Creative Writing and an M.Sc. in Literature and Modernity from the University of Edinburgh, Scotland. He has also studied under Rick Moody at Skidmore College. He's been published in the online poetry journal *Cleaves*, the Edinburgh University Publication *Garlic and Sapphire*, and has been a contributing writer for the *Punxsutawney Spirit* and the travel journal *Exploration*. He was recently published and featured as Author of the Month in the *Missing Slate*. He also writes, records, and performs music throughout New York in a group called the Hudson Underground. Find out more at www.EliotHudson.com.

ALEXIS IVY is a street outreach advocate for the homeless in her hometown, Boston. Her poems have recently appeared in *Spare Change News*, *Eclipse*, *Borderlands*, and *J Journal*. Her first poetry collection *Romance with Small-Time Crooks* was published in 2013 by BlazeVOX [books].

T.R. JONES holds a degree in mathematics from the University of Texas-Austin and is now a graduate student in business at Adams State University. He enjoys spending his free time writing and is nearing completion of his first novel, tentatively titled *The Redemption of Jaxon Collins*.

HANNAH KITTLE is preparing to graduate with an M.A. English from Marshall University, where she has held a position within the program as a teaching assistant. Kittle resides in Huntington, West Virginia. There, she attends classes and manages her photography business of five years. She focuses on creative nonfiction, and more recently, the video essay. You can see Kittle's previous work in the 21st issue of the *Drunken Boat*. A common theme in her work is family. Examining family helps her to understand herself better.

CANDACE LYONS lives in Paris, France. She is a writer and translator.

IRFAN MERCHANT is a poet of Indian origin. He was born in Liverpool and studied medicine in Edinburgh, where he worked as a doctor before leaving to concentrate on poetry, art, and natural healing. His poetry has been published in various and diverse places, including magazines, newspapers, and anthologies, and he is currently studying to become an Ayurvedic practitioner.

IVAN DE MONBRISON is a French poet, writer, and artist who lives in Paris and Marseille. His first poem-novel is *Les Maldormants* (Ressouvenances, 2014). Five poetry chapbooks of his works have been published, including *L'Ombre Déchirée* (La Bartavelle, 1990), *Journal* (La Bartavelle, 1990), and *La Corde à Nu* (La Bartavelle, 1990). His poems and short stories have appeared in literary magazines spanning France, Italy, Belgium, the United Kingdom, Canada, Australia, Switzerland, and the United States.

JENNIFER NEWHOUSE is an Assistant Professor of Creative Writing at Chowan University. She earned her M.F.A. from the University of North Carolina at Greensboro and holds a B.A. Language and Literature from the University of Virginia. Her poems have appeared or are forthcoming in journals such as *SAND*, *Nimrod*, *Salamander*, *Triquarterly*, *Blue Lyra*, and *Canary*.

AYAZ DARYL NIELSEN was born in Valentine, Nebraska; attended schools in Minnesota and Wisconsin; has lived in Monterrey, Mexico and Bonn, Germany; and now lives in Longmont, Colorado with his beloved wife, Judith. A veteran, former hospice nurse, and ex-roughneck (as in oil rigs), he has been the editor of *bear creek haiku* for 25+ years and over 135 issues. He can be found online at *bear creek haiku—poetry, poems and info*. The journal is also a print publication. He is especially delighted by the depth and quality of poets worldwide whose poems have found homes in *bear creek haiku's* online and print presence. His own poetry has been published worldwide and includes "senryu," chosen in 2010 and 2012 as Best of Year by the Irish Haiku Association.

GUNILLA NORRIS lives in Mystic, Connecticut. She is mostly known for her books on the spirituality of the everyday. Her new poetry book is *Joy Is the Thinnest Layer* (Homebound Publishers, 2016). Visit her website GunillaNorris.com or her author page on Facebook.

KORKUT ONARAN is originally from Turkey and now lives in Boulder, Colorado, where he practices architecture and design. He received the First Prize in the Cervena Barva Press 2007 Chapbook Contest and Second Prize in the 2006 Baltimore Review Poetry Competition. His poetry has been published in journals such as *Penumbra, Rhino, Peralta, Colere, Writer's Journal,* and others.

JOSEPH RATHGEBER is an author, poet, and high school English teacher from New Jersey. His short stories and poems have appeared in the *Literary Review, Fourteen Hills, Salamander, J Journal: New Writing on Justice, North Dakota Quarterly, Mizna, Ellipsis,* and elsewhere. His debut story collection is *The Abridged Autobiography of Yousef R. and Other Stories* (ELJ Publications, 2014). He is a five-time Pushcart Prize nominee and received a 2014 Fellowship from the New Jersey State Council on the Arts.

MICHAEL SALCMAN was Chair of the Department of Neurosurgery at the University of Maryland. His collections include *The Clock Made of Confetti* (Orchises Press, 2007), which was nominated for the Poet's Prize, and *The Enemy of Good Is Better* (Orchises Press, 2011). His poems have appeared in *Alaska Quarterly Review, Hopkins Review,* the *Hudson Review, Poet Lore,* and *Rhino. Poetry in Medicine,* his anthology of classic and contemporary poems on doctors and diseases, was recently published by Persea Books in 2015.

NAOMI SHIHAB NYE is the author or editor of more than 25 volumes. She has been a Lannan Fellow, a Guggenheim Fellow, and a Witter Bynner Fellow (Library of Congress). She has received a Lavan Award from the Academy of American Poets, the Isabella Gardner Poetry Award, the Lee Bennett Hopkins Poetry Award, the Paterson Poetry Prize, four Pushcart Prizes, and numerous honors for her children's literature, including two Jane Addams Children's Book Awards. In 2012 she received an Honorable Mention in Poetry from the Arab American National Museum for *Transfer* (BOA Editions, 2011). Her collection *19 Varieties of Gazelle* (Greenwillow Books, 2005) was a finalist for the National Book Award. In January 2010 she was elected to the Board of Chancellors of the Academy of American Poets.

MELVIN STERNE has published 25 stories in magazines of national and international circulation. Several of these stories have won awards. He is the author of a novel, *Zara* (Ink Brush Press, 2012), and a collection of short stories, *The Number You Have Reached* (Lamar University Press, 2013). He recently earned his Ph.D. English from Florida State University and has taught at a number of universities, mainly overseas. He currently lives and writes in Singapore.

Julie Marie Wade is the author of four collections of poetry and four collections of prose. Her latest books include *Catechism: A Love Story* (Noctuary Press, 2016) and *SIX: Poems* (Red Hen Press, 2016), which was selected by C.D. Wright as the winner of the AROHO/To the Lighthouse Poetry Prize. Wade has received an Al Smith Individual Artist Fellowship, a grant from the Barbara Deming Memorial Fund, and the Lambda Literary Award for Lesbian Memoir. She teaches in the creative writing program at Florida International University in Miami. She is married to Angie Griffin and lives in Dania Beach.

Katherine West is the author of *Scimitar Dreams* (Green Fuse Community Press, 2006) and *The Bone Train* (Howling Dog Press, 2008). Her poetry has also appeared in *Earth's Daughters*, *La Petite Zine*, and *Bombay Gin*, among others. In addition to writing, she teaches Tai Chi, Qigong, and improvisational dance to seniors. She believes that organic, expressive, and interactive dance is the most ancient and effective way to achieve (global) healing and community.

Max West is a creative writer, musician, and graduate of U.C. Davis. He has published articles, poems, poetry chapbooks, and a novel. His novel is entitled *Fourteen Months and Two Weeks Downtown: A Fictional Documentary with Names Changed to Protect the Guilty* (Taylor-Dth Publishing (April 2004). He resides in Sacramento, California. More words available at: http://flasheslightning.blogspot.com/

MARK WYATT has been a photographer to the unfamous since 1980. He posts his photographs to mwwyatt.wordpress.com. Deliberate in capturing emotion and composition, the images are never cropped and are minimally processed. Each photograph shows all of what the camera saw and how the camera saw it, at the moment that the shutter was tripped.

LALITAMBA SARANAM

P.O. Box 131, Planetarium Station; New York, NY 10024

Lalitamba partners with Lalitamba Saranam, a holistic homeless shelter in New York City. Through years of working with people in need of permanent housing, we understand how stressful the situation can be. Lalitamba Saranam offers the comforts of home to women in transition, including survivors of domestic violence and runaway youth.

• Social Services

• Life Skills

• Art Studio

• Yoga, Meditation, and Massage

• Clothing Boutique

• Street Outreach

• Soup Kitchen

To make a tax-deductible donation to the shelter, please mail a check to Lalitamba Saranam at the above address. Your generosity makes it all possible. Thank you!

www.threejewelsrefuge.org

SUBSCRIBE

P.O. Box 131, Planetarium Station;
New York, NY 10024

_____$12 One-Year Subscribtion (one annual issue)

_____$20 Two-Year Subscription (two annual issues)

Please include $4.95 for postage and handling and
enclose a check written to *Lalitamba*.

Begin my subscription with issue number _____

Name_____

Address_____

City, State, Zip_____

Please send a gift subscription to:

Begin the subscription with issue number _____

Name_____

Address_____

City, State, Zip_____

CHINTAMANI BOOKS
www.chintamanibooks.org

Chintamani Books is a 501(c)3 non-profit press that was founded to offer book donations to hospital patients, prison inmates, and the homeless population.

We published our first volume at the request of a dedicated group of detox patients at the Addiction Institute, who had experienced our inpatient poetry-and-meditation workshops and wished to study further. Since then, we have grown to offer good reads in fiction, nonfiction, poetry, and translation. Chintamani Books is also the publisher of Lalitamba magazine.

To submit, please send a proposal letter and sample pages/full manuscript in hard copy to:

Lalitamba/Chintamani Books
P.O. Box 131
Planetarium Station
New York, NY 10024

Please include SASE for reply. If you would like your manuscript returned, please provide postage; otherwise, the manuscript will be recycled.

NOTE: Poetry manuscripts should include at least 65 poems/pages.

Take Me (and My Kids)
Last Chance Beach Romance
By
Bonnie Edwards

TAKE ME (AND MY KIDS)

First edition. May 1, 2023.

Copyright © 2023 Bonnie Edwards.

ISBN: 978-1989226193

Written by Bonnie Edwards.